Single's Guide
to
Cruise Vacations

Single's Guide to Cruise Vacations

to

Cruise Vacations

Jacqueline Simenauer
and
Margaret Russell

PRIMA PUBLISHING

PRIMA PUBLISHING and colophon are registered trademarks of Prima Communications, Inc.

Library of Congress Cataloging-in-Publication Data

Simenauer, Jacqueline.
    Single's guide to cruise vacations / Jacqueline Simenauer, Margaret Russell.
        p.   cm.
    Includes index.
    ISBN 0-7615-0324-2
    1. Ocean travel.   2. Cruise ships.   3. Single people—Travel.   I. Russell, Margaret.
II. Title.
G550.R87   1997
910.4'5—dc21   97-27235
                                                                      CIP

97 98 99 00 01 HH 10 9 8 7 6 5 4 3 2 1

Printed in the United States of America

How to Order
Single copies may be ordered from Prima Publishing, P.O. Box 1260BK, Rocklin, CA 95677; telephone (916) 632-4400. Quantity discounts are also available. On your letterhead, include information concerning the intended use of the books and the number of books you wish to purchase.

Visit us online at www.primapublishing.com

To my captain, Peter, and to Tara Heidi, with love and thanks for sailing with me on the high seas of life

To Tillie Himelstein, mother and friend so dearly missed, who lives on forever in our hearts

To Lisa and Lothar Simenauer, whose kindness and generosity have enriched our lives

—J.S.

Contents

Introduction

This book is not *Fodor's*. It is not *Frommer's*. It does not rate the cruise lines. We don't tell you which lines have the largest cabins, the best food, or the greatest entertainment. Other travel and cruise books do that. This book was written for *you*—the single man or woman who is deciding whether to make your next vacation a cruise, and if you do, deciding where you should go and which line you should choose. We know your questions: Am I too old to go? Too young? Will there be any singles on board besides me? Won't I be bored? We also know your doubts: I won't meet anyone. There are too many married couples. The list could continue well past the time you could have boarded the ship!

We've tried to answer many of your questions with this book. We have handpicked thirteen cruise lines to profile because of their popularity among both experienced and first-time cruisers. All offer good values and a wide variety of itineraries for singles to consider when contemplating a cruise. You'll get the inside information as to what you can expect from a cruise, whether it is a relatively short one to the Caribbean or a relatively long one to the Greek islands or Asia. In this book, you will learn the ropes of cruising single. Here is some of what you will pick up:

- How to maneuver yourself to a table in the ship's dining room where other singles are seated
- Where the singles hang out on the ship most of the day and the night

- Which individual bars and/or lounges attract singles
- Which activities attract singles
- How you can use the ship's staff to meet other singles or one particular single to whom you're attracted, and how you can stage the meeting on your own
- The pros and cons of shore excursions; when and where it's dangerous to go ashore by yourself
- The advantages and disadvantages of making major purchases in the ship's shops versus the onshore shops
- Which lines and destinations attract the older singles, the more sophisticated singles, the highly educated singles, or the younger singles
- On which cruise lines you will find dance hosts for single women when dancing is the order of the evening
- Which cruises give price breaks for singles
- Dress and dressing up tips
- Tips on tipping

How did we come up with all this inside information? We talked with the marketing and publicity directors of the major cruise lines about their lines' routines, activities, personalities, and quirks. We tip our sailor's caps to them for their generous gifts of information and time.

Before you reach a final decision on whether you will take a cruise, we urge you to read Chapter 1, "Your Cruise Personality." It should provide a true picture of your psychological, emotional, and physical needs and whether they can be met on a cruise.

Last, but by no means least, keep in mind that your goal on a cruise is not to meet Ms. or Mr. Right but to have the best possible time you can. The rest will follow. Guaranteed.

Single's Guide
to
Cruise Vacations

$\mathcal{Y}$our Cruise Personality

More than four and a half million Americans took a cruise last year. That figure is projected to grow to over seven million per year in the near future. Will that number include you?

Today's ships are floating resorts, utopias at sea. You need never be alone, because thousands of cruisers sail right along with you.

Where would you be happiest sailing? Europe? Alaska? Would the Caribbean suit you? Mexico? How would you like Asia or some offbeat port? Would you be happy on a megaship, a mid-size vessel, or a small ship? Or would you enjoy a true sailing craft, such as the windjammer?

The megaships are truly mammoth in size. Carnival's *Destiny* currently has the reputation of being the world's largest ship, with a passenger capacity of 3,350 people and a crew of over 1,000. It boasts fourteen decks, seventeen bars and lounges, seven restaurants and snack bars, and eighteen elevators. It's so wide that it cannot pass through the Panama Canal; no other ship has that distinction.

Such megaships can amaze the traveler with their awesome size and manifold offerings. You'll find such amenities as an eighteen-hole golf course aboard Royal Caribbean's *Legend of the Seas*. On the *Sun Princess,* you can choose a large-stage Broadway-style production or a simpler cabaret evening. Celebrity's *Galaxy* has an ultramodern spa with three levels of pampering, which comes with a price range of $200 to $699.

Are you concerned that you are too young for cruising, or too old? Or that singles don't cruise? Well, don't be. The average age of cruisers has fallen to forty-nine, according to the Cruise Lines International Association, and the fastest growing cruise population is in the twenty-five to thirty-nine age group. According to statistics, almost one-half of current cruise customers are under forty years of age. Most first-timers are even younger; one-third are single. One in four passengers are singles, sailing with friends. (If that surprises you, consider that over seventy million Americans are single.)

If you think you'd enjoy a cruise, you must decide where you would be most comfortable. Destination will play a part in your choice, but consider as well what sort of ship would best suit you and what sort of company. For instance, if you want entertainment and resortlike facilities, look for a megaship to satisfy your desires. On the other hand, if you are traveling alone and the thought of getting lost among thousands of other passengers makes you feel uncomfortable, you may be happier on a smaller ship. Or you may not want to travel alone at all, in which case you can ask your travel agent to suggest lines that have share programs. Many cruise lines welcome singles and will go so far as to fix you up with a roommate. Not only might you gain a new friend, but you will also pay the lower double-occupancy rate, which can result in substantial savings.

Choosing a destination is a definite consideration. Keep in mind that the megaships usually ply the waters of Alaska, the Caribbean, and Mexico. The smaller ones tend to sail the coasts of Europe and Asia, offering cruises of ten, twelve, or more days.

A CRUISE QUIZ

There are so many points to consider that we feel you would do well to take the following quiz, designed to acquaint you with your cruise personality. Once you know exactly what you want out of a cruise vacation, you can then investigate the array of cruise lines for the one that will best meet your emotional and financial needs.

Personal Concerns

- When is the best time for you to get away from work? You will find more singles cruising in the summertime, if meeting new people is a prime objective.
- How many days do you want to cruise? Consider that in general older singles tend to take the longer cruises.
- Are you looking forward to taking structured onshore tours, or do you crave relaxed outdoor activities?
- Are you the sort who can walk up to a group of people engaged in activity or conversation and just join in? Or would you feel braver with a roommate at your side? If you don't want to sail alone, most lines will make arrangements for you to have a roommate.
- What kind of activities and entertainment do you enjoy as a solo: stage shows, eating, gambling? Is there anything you'll miss out on if you don't have a traveling partner? If you are an older single woman and want to be assured of male companionship, make sure you book a line that has "social" or "gentlemen" hosts. These attractive and distinguished single men, many of whom are retired professionals, range in

age from the forties to sixties (though some are older). They are hired to dance and socialize with you. Lines that have them include: American Hawaii, Holland America, Cunard, Crystal, Delta Queen, Orient, Royal Olympic, Silversea, and World Explorer. These hosts are personable, affable men, and they are good dancers. They have been known to date and subsequently marry some of their passenger-guests, after their tour of duty is over (no dating is allowed on board).

- If you are an older single gentleman, would you like to become a social host and get your cruise free or for a small weekly fee? You can contact the cruise lines directly or contact Lauretta Blake of The Working Vacation, 610 Pine Grove Court, New Lenox, Illinois 60431; telephone (815) 485-8307, fax (815) 485-7142. Applicants are usually aged forty-five to sixty-five. Their dancing ability is evaluated for a $25 fee. If you are hired, your cruise is free, including liquor and laundry allowances and sometimes airfare. Blake's fee is $175 a week. If you get the position directly through the cruise lines, there is no fee. In fact, some lines will pay you to socialize and dance with the women on board. Hosts are not allowed to favor one person or a particular group of people.
- How do you feel about approaching the maitre d' of a ship's dining room to say that you are single and want to be at a table with other singles?
- Are you looking for romance, or are you considering cruising just for the fun of it? If you want a totally single passenger list, see Chapter 13 on Windjammer Barefoot Cruises. It offers singles-only cruises several times a year.
- How willing are you to participate in rather silly activities or games in order to meet new people?
- What type and age of people are you comfortable with? Remember, the more economical the cruise, the more

diversified the passenger list will be, from seniors to college students, from honeymooners to middle-aged couples. The more you pay, the older your fellow passenger tends to be. Upscale cruises get many of the over-fifty-five crowd, especially on lines such as Silversea, Seabourn, Radisson Seven Seas, and Cunard's *Sea Goddess*. Midpriced cruise lines like Celebrity, Royal Caribbean, Princess, and Holland America tend to have more professionals and seniors and fewer families with children.

- Do you want a singles-only cruise? There are many organizations that you can sail with to be assured of singles aboard. Try Single World in Rye, New York, at (800) 223-6490 or Golden Age Travelers in San Francisco, California, at (800) 258-8880. Two newsletters offer advice for those sailing solo: *Travel Companion* in Amityville, New York, at (800) 392-1256 and *The Single Traveler* in Northbrook, Illinois, at (708) 272-6788. Destinations is the name of an exclusive travel club for singles in Florham Park, New Jersey; telephone (201) 660-1111. It organizes cruises for singles from age thirty to fifty. *Maiden Voyages* is a magazine published in San Francisco for women travelers; telephone (800) 528-8425. The Single Persons Travel Club of Rancho Cordova, California, at (800) 865-0732, also arranges cruises for singles.

Size of Ship

- Do you feel more comfortable in big crowds or more intimate atmospheres?
- Are you prone to motion sickness? The bigger the ship, the less motion as it plows the ocean.

Cabin Accommodations

- Will you feel comfortable sharing a cabin, or will you prefer privacy?
- Are you easygoing enough to overlook personal differences if you travel with a roommate—even one you don't know?

Destination

- Do you want sandy beaches galore, water sports, and the sun in your hair, such as you would find in the Caribbean? You will find more younger singles on Caribbean cruises.
- Do you want an intellectually stimulating vacation, full of museums and historic sights, such as you would find in Europe, Alaska, or Asia?

Ship Facilities

- Do you want top-of-the-line luxury, or are you looking for the best you can get for the most economic price?
- Is the quality of the food very important to you? Most lines have excellent food, but the more upscale lines will have food of gourmet quality.
- Are you more likely to get bored on a ship with minimal entertainment? Megaships have more lounges, bars, and nightclubs, which may make it easier for you to meet other people.
- Do you tend to become unnerved by too much glitz and festivity?

- Do you like formality, or are you more at home in a casual atmosphere?
- Do you want a new ship, or will you like the sense of tradition that comes with an older one?
- How important is it that a doctor be available to you? There are usually doctors aboard all ships, but if you have any medical problems—or doubts—check this out first.
- Bottom line: what can you truly afford? If you are on a budget, see Chapter 17, "Best Bets," before you book. These tips can save you almost 50 percent.

Special Information for Gay and Lesbian Travelers

Are you looking for a cruise designed particularly for gay and lesbian travelers? Check with these agencies to learn what voyages are being offered for the gay/lesbian traveler.

Aylson Adventures
PO Box 181223
Boston, MA 02118
(800) 825-9766 or (617) 247-8170

Empress Travel
(800) 429-6969

Located in New York City, Empress specializes in booking cruises for gays and lesbians.

Festive Tours & Travel
(800) 588-4297

Festive is a South Florida firm that offers a regular schedule of one- to four-night gay and lesbian cruises.

Friends Travel
(800) 778-7429

Friends is a California agency that specializes in gay and lesbian cruises.

Pied Piper Travel
330 West 42nd Street
New York, NY 10036
(212) 239-2412; outside New York (800) 874-7312

Pied Piper puts together groups for cruises on the Queen Elizabeth 2.

Olivia Travel
(800) 631-6277

Olivia Travel sponsors four to six full-ship cruises a year for gays and lesbians.

RSVP Travel Productions
2800 University Avenue, S.E.
Minneapolis, MN 55414
(800) 328-7787 or (612) 379-4697

RSVP is a major force in gay cruises. It sells only through travel agents but can be contacted at the address above.

In addition, the names of more than fifty tour operators serving the gay market are listed in a travel calendar published by *Out & About* newsletter for its subscribers. The calendars can be bought for $7 each. Subscription to the newsletter is $49 for ten issues. Contact *Out & About* at 8 West 19th Street, Suite 401, New York, New York 10011; telephone (212) 645-6922.

Now that you have a better idea of what would make your cruise vacation meet all your needs, let's take a closer look at some of America's most popular cruise lines.

$\mathscr{A}$merican Hawaii Cruises

2 N. Riverside Plaza
Chicago, IL 60606
Telephone (312) 466-6000 or (800) 765-7000

Hawaii can be expensive if you're going to see more than one island, especially if you plan to fly between the islands, stay at hotels, and rent cars. Cruising is an excellent way to see it all—or most of it—without the fuss and probably more economically. Restaurant meals alone can be very expensive.

Take American Hawaii's cruise and have no fear of missing any of the major sights—all without spending time in airports or worrying about taxis, luggage, and packing and unpacking.

$\mathscr{G}$ENERAL SHIP INFORMATION

American Hawaii Cruises has one ship, the SS *Independence*, which sails around the Hawaiian islands during a seven-day cruise, departing from the island of Oahu. The *Independence* holds 819 passengers.

Other lines offer cruises of the Hawaiian islands, some of them longer than seven days, but they visit only seasonally. One line sails the islands while repositioning its ship from one of its regular destination points to another. Two others visit from the South Pacific. American Hawaii is the only cruise line that offers seven-day cruises of the Hawaiian islands year-round.

Although the *Independence* is older, an extensive $40 million renovation has restored the classic to its former splendor. "You could call us one of the Grand Old Dames of cruising," says Nancy Lowenherz, director of marketing for American Hawaii Cruises. But Lowenherz cautions, "Keep in mind that this is not a glitzy megaship like those that ply the Caribbean. The people who come on board really do come for the destinations and the experience. We try to give them a little extra, in terms of what we provide on board—the entertainment, the activities—but the ship itself is not the destination."

Lowenherz also suggests that "if you compare us, the ticket price is quite a bit higher than a lot of the Caribbean cruise lines, even some of the more upscale ones. But compared to a land-based vacation in Hawaii, chances are we're going to be very competitive."

ACCOMMODATIONS FOR SINGLES

American Hawaii doesn't cater to singles but does welcome them. The cruises are aimed at the financially secure cruise customer, probably a bit older and more apt to travel farther from home. The *Independence* has twenty single-occupancy cabins. They book for the regular double-occupancy fare. Single-occupancy cabins book early and are not always available. Single supplements, which range from 33 percent to 100 percent more, are charged for a double-occupancy cabin occupied by one person.

The interior of each cabin is different, including the placement of beds. You can choose to have a queen- or king-size bed or a pull-down bunk. Double-occupancy cabins are naturally bigger than the singles, which tend to be very small and are not in the upper sections; while you may save some money, you will not get as spacious a cabin. To have more room or a cabin on one of the upper decks, you'll have to pay the supplement or find a roommate.

The *Independence* was built for a variance of three classes, so there are several different sizes of accommodations. The smallest cabins were eventually designated as singles, though they're not all uniform. In fact, throughout the ship, every cabin is different from its neighbor. This makes for some very unusual shapes.

Many of the fixtures are original 1950s, adding to the ship's Art Deco decor. "We're not old-world luxury," Lowenherz says, "but we do have a lot of the character lacking in a newer ship."

A particular opportunity exists for single parents who want to travel with their children. The year-round policy is that children under the age of eighteen cruise free when sharing a cabin with two full-fare passengers. Single parents traveling with their children will still have to pay the supplement, but the kids then share the cabin for free. This makes for a quite reasonable vacation when you consider that all meals are included and all the kids' entertainment is on board. The only thing not included are shore excursions, and even then American Hawaii has special children's rates and activities, such as a summer program that arranges chaperoned beach parties.

PASSENGER INFORMATION

Passengers on the *Independence* tend to be older—fifty-five and over, as a rule. However, during the mid-June to mid-August summer vacation season, the ship gets lots of children on board, lowering the average age significantly. Families travel during the summer, and you might find as many as 150 kids aboard.

"We're not actively going after the singles market," Lowenherz reminds us, yet just by the nature of the product, the *Independence* attracts them anyway. "It's interesting," she says, "we attract more single women than men. Single women tend to travel by themselves with much more comfort than single men. If I were going to Hawaii as a single woman, I think I would prefer to be on a cruise ship than in a hotel. There's much more opportunity to meet and interact with people on a ship than alone in a hotel where you don't have anybody encouraging you to participate or introduce you."

ONBOARD LIFE

Dress is casual on board. Bring a cover-up for the inevitable swimsuit. If you have any aloha attire, like a muumuu or Hawaiian shirt, that's always fun. By the way, these days muumuus are not big tents; there are some very pretty ones. Many sundresses are available in pretty Hawaiian patterns. Bring some fun, brightly colored clothing.

Each cruise holds a captain's dinner, which is moderately formal. The men generally wear a coat and tie or sometimes just a coat. Women wear a dress or a skirt and blouse. Some passengers like to dress up more than others. Suit yourself. Truly formal wear is not a requirement.

There are two seatings in the dining room, and because passengers tend to be older, the first seating is the preferred one. The older crowd wants to get ready for the next day's activities. Passengers tend to rise early and be off and doing something. Many of the tours leave at 8:00 A.M. Also, when passengers return to the ship after a busy day, they're tired. This is not a late-night party kind of cruise. You won't find a single disco on board the *Independence*, though there is late-night dancing.

Every morning, there is a mile-long deck walk and an exercise class. The ship offers an exercise room with machines such as a Universal gym, treadmill, bicycles, and step machines. Those who aren't interested in such fitness activities can always find a deck chair and be perfectly happy.

A surprising number of people never leave the ship. "It's kind of crazy," says Lowenherz, "but we have some repeaters who come on board just to enjoy being in the warm sun and hang out on the ship. They take part in the activities we offer during the day, but they don't go ashore."

The majority do take advantage of the shore excursions, however. In most ports, the ship anchors dockside, making it easy for passengers to come and go. There are no customs or immigration, so when the ship arrives in port there is no waiting before you can get off. The only thing passengers must wait for is the gangway to go down!

BEST BETS FOR MEETING PEOPLE

As with any vacation or trip, it's a good idea to participate in as much as you possibly can when you're on your own. That's the way to meet more people and have more fun. Go to the cruise director and tell him or her you're by yourself and would like to meet other singles aboard. Let the maitre d' know you're by yourself and would like to dine with other singles.

The crew is conscientious when it comes to helping singles meet new people. Lowenherz says, "If they know that you're by yourself, they definitely will make an effort to introduce you to people and try and encourage you to participate."

On Big Band cruises, as many as four male dance hosts will be available as partners for single women passengers.

*I*TINERARY AND SEA SIGHTS

The islands are fairly close together and most sailing takes place at night, but the *Independence* seldom enters or exits a port unless it is daylight, for safety considerations. You'll never be farther than a couple of hours away from one of the islands.

The ship departs on Saturday evenings. Sunday is a full day at sea. In pleasant weather, the ship circumnavigates the island of Kauai and passes by the famous Napoli coastline, which is inaccessible other than by sea or by air. The sea cliffs there are a spectacular two thousand feet high.

On Sunday evening, the ship arrives at Willy-Willy, on the island of Kauai, where it stays Sunday night and all day Monday. It departs Monday evening and heads for two full days at the port of Kahalue, Maui. On Tuesday morning, it docks at Maui at 8:00 A.M. It overnights there and departs Wednesday at 5:00 P.M.

On Thursday at 8:00 A.M., the ship arrives in Hilo, on the big island of Hawaii. Hilo is the jumping-off point for Volcano National Park, where the volcano Kilawaue has been consistently active since 1983. Departure from Hilo is at 6:00 P.M.

On Friday, the ship visits Kona, on the other side of Hawaii—the dryer, sunnier side. Here, passengers may enjoy snorkeling, deep-sea fishing, or the beaches, for which the area is famous.

Early Saturday morning, the ship arrives back in its Honolulu home port.

*S*HORE EXCURSIONS

The *Independence* is in port virtually every day, and a huge variety of shore excursions are available. In fact, in 1996, *Travel Holiday* magazine named these excursions "the best of the best."

More than fifty different shore excursions take passengers almost anywhere they might want to go on the islands. They range from as active as you can imagine to as relaxed and comfortable as you want to feel. Some make use of motor coaches. Some are on horseback. You can explore via plane, bicycle, hiking trails, or scuba gear. There are even parasail opportunities. Just about any mode of transportation available can be experienced in Hawaii. Basic sightseeing tours cover all the main attractions and points of interest. Other excursions might not show you a lot of the island, but you will have a unique experience horseback riding or taking a kayak trip. In short, there are excursions to appeal to just about any interest.

On Monday, the ship doesn't leave until four in the afternoon, so that makes a good day for golfing. Golfers can get a very early morning tee time and can either bring clubs or rent them. Hawaii has some of the best golfing in the world.

A good bet for the first-timer is the Captain's Choice, a grouping of shore excursions for each port that will give you a very good overview of Hawaii. A slight discount is available when purchasing these as a package.

There is also a series called "Hawaiionic" tours and hikes. The number of people on these are limited to about twenty to twenty-four per group. They're designed to be much more personal and are much more intensive in terms of what tour members will see and do. For example, on the volcano hike, tour members actually hike down into the crater of one of the 1950 Kiloua eruptions. It's a six-mile trek, and though not particularly strenuous, members do have to be in decent physical condition to handle it. You wouldn't have to be a veteran hiker—some people have done it in sandals. Yet it's certainly more adventurous than, say, a bus tour.

Another example is a hike that will take you into Maui's rain forest. This hike is guided by a naturalist, who will explain the varieties of plants and how the ancient Hawaiians used them as food, medicine, or tools. The naturalist guide will talk about what's indigenous to the islands and what was brought in by others. This walk provides an extensive history of the islands.

These specialized tours are designed to be more educational, so you can learn something about the environment, the people, and the history of the area, whether it is Kauai, Maui, or the big island. There is at least one Hawaiionic tour in each port.

The cruise line also offers helicopter flights called Flight See, which are popular. They offer a unique way to see the islands by flying over areas otherwise inaccessible. The scenery is incredibly beautiful.

You can also design your own jaunts, renting a car on any of the islands and exploring on your own, at your own pace. American Hawaii works with all the major rental car companies and will provide you with maps and suggestions of where to go.

Whichever tours or activities you choose, you'll find out quickly that Hawaii is much more than beaches. Cruise passengers are amazed at how much there is to see and do and learn. The history of the Hawaiian people, going back to ancient times, is fascinating. Their spiritualism and traditions make an absorbing study. American Hawaii Cruises tries to present that in its cruise experience.

ᐯ ERSONAL SAFETY

For those who want to venture ashore alone, it's obviously good practice to be aware of your surroundings, wherever you are. Hawaii is a state of the United States, so there is no language problem, and all of the various safety considerations you would find anywhere in the U.S. are in place. "I would say that it's safe to be by yourself," says Lowenherz. The islands are not known for crime. Those who rent a car should lock the doors when leaving it parked.

Don't leave valuables in the open. Don't leave your towel on the beach with all of your belongings. In general, practice the same common sense that you would anywhere.

Lowenherz gives these tips and suggestions for singles going ashore solo: "We arrive in Kauai at about four or five o'clock on Sunday afternoon. There's not really much within walking distance, so I wouldn't suggest walking into town at night. However, taxis are available."

THEME AND SPECIAL-INTEREST CRUISES

On American Hawaii's Big Band cruises, as many as four gentlemen social hosts are on board. The cruise line will do five or six of these cruises in 1998. For most of them, the music will be provided by the Sammy Kaye Orchestra (that is subject to change). These cruises are very popular.

The Aloha Festival, a statewide Hawaiian gala commemorating Hawaiian culture, lasts the entire month of September. On board the *Independence*, all Hawaiian activities and entertainment will be amplified in the spirit of the celebration.

In addition, whale watching cruises take place from January through March.

CRUISING SEASONS

If your travel schedule is flexible, it makes a lot of sense to go during the off-season when fewer families and children travel. Hawaii is truly a year-round destination, and there is no official off-season, but two months out of the year, May and September, seem a little softer than the rest.

In general, Lowenherz recommends that singles avoid Christmas, New Year's, and Easter vacations. The holidays, particularly Easter, tend to be very popular for family groups.

SPECIAL PACKAGES AND ADD-ONS

While American Hawaii doesn't generally offer discounts, it does have several value-added packages, such as a nine-day vacation. In cooperation with hotels such as the Outriggers, it offers a nine-day vacation that includes two free days in a hotel. This might be limited to Oahu, or the offer might be extended to the island of your choice, depending on the package. Sometimes a rental car will be included. If you're on another island, perhaps inter-island air transportation will be included. Some special package deals allow you to combine your cruise with three nights in Hawaii or Maui.

A golf program is available. Before your cruise, your travel agent and the cruise line can arrange for your tee time at the island golf courses of your choice.

NEW AND FUTURE POSSIBILITIES

This fall, American Hawaii will initiate a program with Hawaiian Airlines, in which passengers who depart from West Coast cities will get a free upgrade to first class.

CHAPTER 3

*C*arnival
Cruise Lines

3655 N.W. 87th Avenue
Miami, FL 33178
Telephone (305) 599-2600 or (800) 227-6482

Calling themselves "the most popular cruise line in the world," Carnival boasts a fleet of superliners and megaliners as well as traditional ships. With lavish facilities, a new fleet, large cabins, and good value, Carnival is the place to be if you like plenty of action and glitz. "We are the largest cruise line by a variety of measures," says Jennifer de La Cruz, public relations manager of Carnival Cruise Lines. "We carry more passengers than any other cruise line in the world. We're more profitable. And currently, I believe, we have more ships than anybody else as well."

*G*ENERAL SHIP INFORMATION

Carnival developed the Fun Ship concept, offering nonstop activities appealing to people of all ages and backgrounds. Eleven ships make up the Carnival fleet, including the Carnival *Destiny*, the world's first 100,000-ton cruise ship. Within the fleet, Carnival currently has 17,690 berths, based on double occupancy. That doesn't even include the upper berths.

The onboard equipment in the fleet is basically the same from ship to ship. Activities are the same. Food and entertainment are the same. There are different classes of vessels, however. The Fantasy class is a little larger and has more extensive health and fitness facilities. The *Tropical*, the smallest ship in the fleet, offers the most diverse itinerary. If you're looking for a Carnival Alaskan cruise, it will be on the *Tropical*. If you're looking for a seven-day cruise out of Florida, you have a few options.

The Fantasy class ships are virtually identical. So are the Holiday class ships, which are the ships from the 1980s. Of this class, there are three ships. They're slightly smaller and they don't have as elaborate a health and fitness facility, but otherwise they're very similar to the Fantasy class ships. The differences are pretty subtle; for example, the Holiday class ships have fewer bars and lounges.

Carnival is in a category known in the industry as the "contemporary" market, as opposed to a premium cruise line like Holland America or an upscale cruise line like Silversea. "We're at the other end," says de La Cruz. "We're a mass-market, mainstream-type cruise line."

DESTINATIONS, LENGTH OF CRUISES, DEPARTURE PORTS

Carnival ships cruise year-round to the Bahamas and Caribbean and the U.S. West Coast/Mexican Riviera. You'll also find them seasonally in the Panama Canal, Hawaii, and Alaska. Carnival is primarily a Bahamas, Caribbean, and Mexican Riviera cruise operator. These destinations are the mainstays of its cruise packages. Voyages usually take seven days or less.

Carnival cruises appeal to people with limited time—those many, many Americans who opt for the long weekend or the shorter, more frequent vacations over the traditional one-week or two-week vacations. For singles on a limited budget or with a limited amount of time, three- and four-day cruises are the perfect answers. Three of the ships offer three- and four-day cruises, which are also great for people who have never taken a cruise before and just want to get their feet wet and try it out. These shorter voyages go to the Bahamas from Florida. Sailing out of Los Angeles, they also cruise the Pacific coast of Mexico. Carnival also has one route that sails to Cozumel in Mexico on a four-day cruise.

The remainder of the ships offer seven-day cruises to the Caribbean, the Mexican Riviera, or Alaska. They sail to Alaska in the summer, occasionally sail through the Panama Canal, and have a limited number of Hawaii voyages, which is new this year. The principal packages of the cruise program are the three-, four-, and seven-day cruises.

"We have, I believe, one of the newest fleet of cruise ships in the industry," says de La Cruz. The oldest ship in Carnival's fleet was launched in 1982. Six ships were launched in the 1990s. Those were the Fantasy class ships, 2,040-passenger vessels with seven-deck glass atriums, huge health and fitness facilities, large casinos and show lounges, and lots and lots of deck space so passengers could either be in the midst of the action or sit and read a book in peace and quiet. That availability of choice is the real advantage of a larger ship.

Most of Carnival's ships are superliners. Those built from the mid-1980s on accommodate upwards of 1,400 passengers. Only one ship is of a smaller class: the *Tropical* sails to Alaska and is just a summer program; while repositioning from one ocean to the other, it typically transits the Panama Canal.

$\mathscr{A}$CCOMMODATIONS FOR SINGLES

Singles aged fifty and over are eligible for Carnival's expanded discount program. To qualify, singles must be members of the American Association of Retired Persons (AARP). For an extremely modest yearly membership fee, the AARP single can save more than $200 on selected cruises.

Carnival ships are not outfitted with single cabins. They never have been. While different types of travelers can book into the double-occupancy cabin; only one type of traveler can book into a single-occupancy cabin. "It's just not practical to build a ship that way," says de La Cruz.

Singles need to consider what sort of cabin arrangement they're seeking and to evaluate their budgets. Carnival offers a share program, in which singles are matched with same-sex roommates. The program tries to put people in similar age groups and pair smokers with smokers and nonsmokers with nonsmokers. It can make no guarantees, but the company does give its best effort. If you are willing to give the program a try, it's a very good value.

If you want a cabin to yourself, you will have to pay a supplement. On certain sailings, the supplement is 150 percent of the fare; otherwise, the single supplement will be 200 percent. This means you're going to pay for two people to have your own cabin.

Many singles avail themselves of the share program. The pricing differs based on whether you opt for a double share, a triple share, or a quad share. The quad share puts four people in a cabin. Occasionally, a quad share cabin will sail with fewer than four people in the cabin. It does happen. When booking a quad share, though, you should assume that you will be with three other people. Depending on how the numbers work out, you may get lucky and share with less than three others. Sometimes there will only be two of you. It all depends on how many people book the share program on that sailing. Each one gets the rate for the designated share asked for. The fewer people sharing a cabin, the more expensive it will be. Overall, the share program means a good savings over what singles would pay to have a cabin with no companions. A knowledgeable travel agent who specializes in cruising should be able to help you decide.

The share program is for the cruise only, which means it doesn't include airfare, although air add-ons are available. You can also look into getting transfers from the cruise line. If you book the air/sea package through Carnival, the transfers are automatically included. If you don't book the air/sea package, you can still purchase Carnival's transfer option, in which you're greeted at the airport and taken to the port via a bus. Having this escort for transfer offers a certain amount of comfort for single travelers.

"We welcome singles," says de La Cruz. "We don't specifically market to singles, but then we don't have to, because by now everyone associates us with the singles crowd."

PASSENGER INFORMATION

The median age on a three- and four-day cruise is early forties. On seven-day cruises, the median age is midforties. Canal transits attract passengers a little older, from the fifty- to sixty-year range.

Carnival cruises carry lots of children and lots of seniors. "In fact," says de La Cruz, "we carry more people over the age of

fifty-five than any upscale cruise line that's catering to them."
This claim comes simply from the shear volume of people on the
ships. And just because someone is older doesn't mean that he or
she wants a cruise oriented to the older person. There are many
young-at-heart people who like the casualness, the activity, and
the entertainment on a Carnival cruise. The slower pace and style
of the upscale lines don't appeal to all older passengers.

The three- and four-day cruises are more popular for younger
singles. The shorter length of these cruises, interestingly, increases
the pace on board. By and large, this pace is set by the passengers, so the tempo tends to be a little faster on shorter cruises
because there's less time to get it all in. On a seven-day cruise,
passengers tend to start more slowly. The shorter the cruise, the
more likely the passengers will jump into the activities and really
get into the groove of the cruise experience. It's the measure of
the passenger's state of mind.

The shorter cruises to the Bahamas or the Caribbean attract
younger people who generally have limited budgets. These
cruises are more affordable to someone just starting out in a
career, who may have less flexibility in terms of both money and
vacation time.

ONBOARD LIFE

There is usually a very convivial, casual atmosphere on cruises,
but this is particularly noticeable on Carnival cruises. In the dining room, Carnival's staff tries to put singles together, although
they can't guarantee that service—it simply doesn't always work
out. But they make their best effort. You can check with the maitre
d' when you board and ask what other sorts of folks are going to
be at your table. Ask if you can be placed at a table for singles, if

you're not already. There is a limit to the flexibility that's possible, but it certainly doesn't hurt to ask.

On a typical cruise, after boarding and settling into their cabins, perhaps meeting their roommate(s) if they have booked a share program, most people will try to orient themselves to the ship. Activities don't get going until midafternoon on the first day, allowing time for this transition from land to sea life. The ship layouts are relatively easy to learn.

Next, passengers have something to eat. For those into health and fitness, Carnival's ships have excellent health and fitness facilities, particularly the Fantasy class ships. The newer ships have 12,000-square-foot spas. There is no cost to use the Nautilus equipment, the sauna, or the steam room. But you should remember to sign up early for the spa services you want.

Activities usually start about three o'clock in the afternoon. There is an orientation talk, and the spa usually offers a familiarization talk. You'll find all activities listed in the onboard newsletter, *Carnival Capers*. A copy should be in your cabin when you board. If not, be sure to ask for your copy.

Many of the activities are designed so that you don't need to be traveling with anyone else. The activities don't focus on partners or couples, which could make singles feel awkward. A lot of the activities are group endeavors, making it unimportant if you happen to be traveling by yourself. Carnival does not supply dance hosts, because they are not seen as necessary. The atmosphere on a Carnival cruise is such that passengers can meet other people with relative ease.

Carnival assumes that everybody is there for the same purpose: everybody is on vacation, and everybody is there to meet other people. This is really the most exciting and rewarding aspect of taking a cruise; the people you meet can be the most enriching part of the vacation. Carnival emphasizes this mind-set while many resorts or hotels may not. "In the hotel," says de La Cruz, "people are often there on business. Some are just passing through overnight. They're not there to meet other people. They're not there necessarily for a vacation." Even at a resort, people generally stay to themselves. That tends not to happen on a cruise.

Activities on Carnival cruises go from dawn to dusk. You'll be introduced to a lot of deck games. Activities are conducted from the stage of the main pool area. If you're really daring, you can volunteer for one of them. Otherwise, you can stand back and have fun with all the other people gathered around the pool to watch. These activities are often hysterical.

On the other hand, some people board a cruise ship seeking a genuine mental break. They want to sit outside and read a book. For them that is the ultimate enjoyment. Carnival's staff feels that this is also perfectly fine.

Here is a typical schedule on a Carnival cruise. Breakfast service starts at 6:30 A.M. Spa activities start at 7:00 A.M. The slot machines in the casino are ready for action at 8:00 A.M. Shuffleboard is available from 9:00 A.M. The library opens at 9:30 A.M. The Ping-Pong tournament starts at 10:00 A.M., along with the full casino. At 10:30 A.M., the photo gallery opens. There is horse racing at 11:00 A.M.

Then lunch gets going, followed by talent show registration. Passengers can enjoy an ice carving demonstration, a slot tournament, a dance class, tours of the galley, cooking lessons and food carving, and jackpot bingo.

In the late afternoon, passengers listen to a debarkation briefing or a port briefing. Then the passengers can attend the cocktail reception for the early and late dinner seatings. Music starts kicking up in certain areas on the ship, such as the promenade and the piano bar. Guests enjoy show entertainment, all the bars are going, and there's more bingo.

Aboard a Carnival ship, casual is the order of the day, except for dinner. During the day, shorts and T-shirts are fine, even in the ports of call. Dinner may require slacks or a sundress on casual nights. Depending on whether you're on a three-, four-, or seven-day cruise, there will be one to two formal nights. These occasions call for cocktail attire.

BEST BETS FOR MEETING PEOPLE

Carnival Cruise Lines carries more passengers than any other line in the world. You're bound to meet lots of people. To meet the most singles possible, be sure to attend the first night's singles party that is held on all cruises. The cruise director will announce it with drums and whistles. You'll also find the time and place listed in the *Carnival Capers* newsletter. This offers a tremendous opportunity to meet fellow single passengers. Some couples attend as well. "It's a great way to meet other people, particularly to pinpoint other single people on the ship," says de La Cruz.

The gym is a good place to talk to people. Carnival offers lots of other activities, geared to different levels. A variety of games are offered, from bingo to horse racing to trivia contests, which you can simply go to and participate. Even people who are traveling with others can enter these activities by themselves. The activities encourage you to have fun with the people around you. There are wine and cheese tastings. Again, you can attend and be comfortable and initiate conversation with other folks, or you can simply enjoy the activity.

Carnival's de La Cruz recommends that singles not go on board expecting to find a love interest or romance, because they may be setting themselves up for disappointment. If it happens, it happens. The worst thing a single traveler can do is anticipate romance.

"It typically pops up when and where you least expect it. I think you should approach a cruise with a mind-set of meeting interesting people and finding some relaxation and enjoyment, but not necessarily finding romance."

If you want to interact with other people and make new friends, however, the best way is to get involved in the activities. Carnival personnel like to joke that you shouldn't worry—you're never going to see any of these people again. This can release a lot of people's inhibitions, which can be a good thing. You needn't be shy about initiating conversations and participating in activities, because the vast majority of people will be very warm and open to including you into their spectrum of friends and traveling mates.

If you'd like to be introduced to a particular person, you can approach the social host or the cruise director. These officials wear badges and an outfit that distinguishes them. The cruise director is very visible during the cruise. You'll know who he or she is. The cruise director and the social host will be the ones running all the activities. They'll help you out with meeting someone, although obviously they can't be matchmakers. You can also tell them that you're trying to meet other people your age.

SHORE EXCURSIONS

Shore excursions are geared to the individual passenger's interests. As a single traveler, you should be quite comfortable going on excursions with other guests. After all, everyone on the excursion is experiencing the same cruise, the same vacation, the same ship. So you automatically have a common starting point for conversation.

Snorkeling is a great thing to do in the Bahamas and the Caribbean, particularly for those who haven't done it before. Also, scuba diving is available. The most popular tours are the basic city tours. People usually want to become familiar with an island they are visiting for the first time. They want to see the highlights in the most practical way possible. Carnival offers a two-hour city tour, leaving time in which you can go back and revisit and explore things you found of particular interest.

While shopping ashore, compare prices. The gift shops aboard the ships do run sales and specials on certain items, usually each day. There are some really good deals to be had. Price jewelry, perfume, and other items before you leave home, again when you get on board, and when you go into the ports.

PERSONAL SAFETY

Safety cautions depend on the port of call. The cruise director will provide insight during port briefings about which destinations may require extra discretion. In a port like St. Thomas, probably the most popular cruise port in the Caribbean, you can comfortably walk off the ship alone and take a taxi to the beach. Or you can grab a tram service over to Charlotte Amalie, the huge shopping area in St. Thomas. In a port like Caracas, the shipboard personnel might strongly recommend that a single woman take an escorted shore excursion provided by the cruise line.

CRUISING SEASONS

For young singles, springtime is by far the most popular cruising time on a Carnival ship, because a lot of young people are on college vacations. During the summer, there is a good mix of ages. More children will be on board during the summer, but there will still be a broad mix of people. After all, summer is vacation time for virtually everyone, and it is Carnival's busiest season. It's also the most expensive time to cruise, because it is high season, when everybody takes a vacation.

Winter is also considered high season, but not as high as summer. Fall is the most value-oriented time to cruise. Again, there will be a broad mix of passengers in the fall.

PRECRUISE INFORMATION

When asked for precruise advice, Carnival representatives say the one mistake that people typically make is to overpack for a cruise. You do not want to run out of clothes, but you should also be careful not to overpack. Plan your outfits day to day and make a list as you pack. It will help you plan. Then throw in no more than one or two extra things, and leave it at that.

NEW AND FUTURE POSSIBILITIES

Carnival *Destiny* holds 2,600 passengers in double-occupancy cabins and 3,350 people total. At the present time it is the largest cruise ship in service in the world.

The *Destiny* sports a food court, with several areas serving different types of cuisine, including a pizzeria, an Asian specialty area, an Italian area, an American area serving burgers, hot dogs, and sandwiches, and a huge salad bar (which Carnival has on all its ships). The food court is open during the day, and the pizzeria is open twenty-four hours. No other ship has anything like this.

Evidently, a majority of people don't want the formality of going to the dining room for lunch and breakfast. Carnival found that about 70 percent of its passengers were eating breakfast and lunch in the indoor/outdoor cafe area rather than in the main dining room, so it began beefing up these areas.

The two dining rooms are double-deckers, with two seatings for dinner: early and late.

The Carnival *Destiny* is in a class all its own. It is so wide it cannot pass through the Panama Canal! The ship boasts seventeen bars and lounges, many entertainment venues, and eighteen elevators. There are also more people, but the design flow on this ship is the best in the fleet, to accommodate the greater numbers. More people should not make the ship feel more crowded; on the contrary, it should feel a bit less so.

The onboard offerings are consistent with the rest of the fleet. The difference is in the size of the spa: it is the largest ever. The show lounge is extraordinary, with performances that delight audiences. There is even a sports bar, a new feature on a Carnival ship, with lots of sports programming via satellite.

CHAPTER 4

*C*elebrity Cruises

5201 Blue Lagoon Drive
Miami, FL 33126
Telephone (305) 262-8322 or (800) 437-3111

Started in 1989, Celebrity Cruises is a newcomer to the industry. The company set out to deliver luxury cruises at prices affordable to experienced travelers, and they have done it. Celebrity was given the award for top value from the authoritative *Fielding Cruises 1995*. It was the top premium cruise line rated by the *Berlitz Guide to Cruising*. It was rated as one of the top ten cruise lines by readers of *Travel and Leisure* magazine. With their five sleek ships, Celebrity offers deluxe quality at moderate prices.

*G*ENERAL SHIP INFORMATION

Celebrity Cruises uses five ships, including the *Century*, which holds 1,750 passengers, and the *Galaxy*, which holds 1,870. The two are sister ships. Celebrity has plans to bring out the *Mercury* shortly, and this will be another sister ship to the *Galaxy*. Celebrity's ships are ultramodern and the cabins spacious.

DESTINATIONS, LENGTH OF CRUISES, DEPARTURE PORTS

All of Celebrity's ports of call are exciting. The cruise line is offering premium cruises of seven to sixteen nights in length, sailing to the Caribbean, Bermuda, Alaska, transcanal, coastal, and South American itineraries. Celebrity also has two ships on the New York to Bermuda run.

PASSENGER INFORMATION

Younger travelers tend to choose Caribbean sailings, while older singles gravitate toward Alaskan voyages. However, any given Celebrity cruise contains a cross-section of guests representing all age categories. "As far as attracting singles, we feel that the destination plays a more active role in determining our guests than the specific vessel they choose," says Helen Burford, vice president of marketing and communications at Celebrity Cruises.

ONBOARD LIFE

Under the direction of their award-winning French chef, Michael Roux, Celebrity has become known for its superior cuisine and service. Chef Roux has created menus and selected wine lists for all the ships, continuing Celebrity's award-winning heritage of offering some of the finest cuisine at sea. Passengers with special requests can order vegetarian, diabetic, low-sodium, low-cholesterol, kosher, "lean and light," or children-friendly meals.

Throughout Celebrity's sailings, a variety of attire is acceptable for dinner. There are casual, informal, and formal evenings.

For example, a seven-night cruise includes three casual nights, two informal nights, and two formal nights. The recommended dress is listed in the ship's daily published programs, which are slipped under your door every night.

After dinner, guests usually go directly to the Show Lounge Theater to see the evening's main entertainment. After that, there are options galore: a casino, nightclub, disco, specialty bars/ lounges, and shops. Follow your instincts and follow the crowd.

For single women passengers, Celebrity has at least two and sometimes as many as six social hosts on board during the fleet's longer itineraries, including the Panama Canal, the Ultimate Caribbean, the Alaska, and the South America cruises. Hosts are typically gentlemen between fifty-five and sixty-five years of age, and they are carefully screened before being engaged on any of the vessels. They must be proficient dancers and are available to escort guests on land tours if requested and when space permits.

Some onboard lounges attract singles in particular, for example, Celebrity's trendsetting Michael's Club, a cigar bar. There is also a martini bar and a champagne and caviar bar. These are popular with single guests on all of Celebrity's ships. Sports activities, social mixers, deck parties, enrichment programs, and dancing till dawn are also very popular.

A 10,000-square-foot, high-tech spa is available on the *Century*, which offers treatments and therapies currently unavailable on any other cruise vessel. The spa offers three levels of pampering, ranging in price from $200 to $699. For golfers, Celebrity's golf simulator is available on board the *Galaxy* and *Century*.

Every ship provides a daily listing of activities and events on board. You can get involved in as many as you wish, especially while the ships are at sea. Activities range from fitness classes to wine tastings, from art auctions to cigar rolling demonstrations. Travelers may also opt to do nothing but relax and enjoy the cruise.

Celebrity's Family Cruising Program entertains children with organized daily activities for four age groups, allowing parents to enjoy some•quiet time during the cruise in addition to quality time with their children.

ⒷEST BETS FOR MEETING PEOPLE

Traveling by yourself or taking a friend on a cruise is a personal choice, and no one way is necessarily better. Some singles like to travel by themselves to get time alone, away from their usual hectic lifestyles. Others choose to travel with a friend in order to have a companion throughout the duration of the cruise.

As a single person, you make the decision whether you want to be alone or you want to socialize. Cruise ships are a terrific place to meet people—at your pace and in a safe environment—but you won't meet a soul if you spend all your time in your stateroom. Get out early and start networking with fellow guests. Long-standing friendships (and possibly romance) are sure to follow.

A single person should speak to the maitre d'. Those who share the same interests and marital status are usually seated together. A single who approaches the maitre d' on the first day of the cruise is most certain to be seated with other singles, often with those who share similar interests. The cruise director organizes events and activities for single guests. One way to get acquainted with other guests is to attend the singles party given at the beginning of each cruise.

Apart from the many singles mixers organized by the cruise director on board each cruise, there is no specific area where singles hang out. In general, it is a good idea to spend time in popular areas, such as the pool area by day and the disco by night. Above all, don't be shy and do not sit alone in a dark corner. Look for groups you think you might get along with, introduce yourself, and join them. That's the great part about being on a cruise. Unlike in a big city, the camaraderie and sense of community created aboard a cruise ship is unique, and a single will be welcomed into many shipboard "families" with open arms.

Typically, singles migrate to the lounge with live music before dinner and to the late-night nightclub or disco after dinner. Keep your eyes open, use your common sense, and follow the crowd.

SHORE EXCURSIONS

Shore excursions are one of the best ways to meet other people on a cruise vacation, and travelers should try to book their outings as soon as the shore excursion desk opens. This is usually the first night. The more popular excursions may be sold out if you book late. Celebrity offers a variety of excursions.

PERSONAL SAFETY

Celebrity advises guests to bring some cash; however, guests are definitely encouraged to carry most of their funds in the form of traveler's checks and credit cards.

CRUISING SEASONS

Celebrity advises singles to avoid Christmas, New Year's, and Easter holiday cruises, as well as summer sailings. These dates tend to attract families and couples.

$\mathcal{T}$IPPING

Celebrity maintains a tipping guideline of about $70 per passenger for seven days.

$\mathcal{N}$EW AND FUTURE POSSIBILITIES

In 1998, the Celebrity fleet will be adding South Pacific and Europe to its destinations.

CHAPTER 5

*C*lipper
Cruise Line

7711 Bonhomme Avenue
St. Louis, MO 63105
Telephone (314) 727-2929;
outside Missouri, (800) 325-0010

Clipper cruises provide access to areas of natural beauty and cultural interest, giving travelers a profound sense of place in destinations as diverse as the hidden fjords of Alaska and serene Caribbean coves, the antebellum South along the Intracoastal Waterway, and the whale-crossed waters of the Sea of Cortez and the Bay of Fundy.

"Our mission statement," says Elizabeth Raven McQuinn, public relations manager for Clipper Cruise Line, "is to find discerning travelers who want to see places of natural beauty and cultural interests. We have access into secluded waterways the bigger ships could never consider. We do have competition—there are other cruise lines that sail small ships that go on unusual itineraries. But not many."

GENERAL SHIP INFORMATION

Clipper Cruise Line's two U.S. flagships, the 100-passenger *Nantucket Clipper* and the 138-passenger *Yorktown Clipper*, cruise the waterways of the Americas, from Alaska's Inside Passage to Costa Rica, Panama, the Grenadines, and the Leeward and Windward Islands, and from Canada's Bay of Fundy to the Virgin Islands.

"Our ships are very nice," says McQuinn, "but our focus is on where we're going."

DESTINATIONS, LENGTH OF CRUISES, DEPARTURE PORTS

Basically, Clipper cruises focus more on the destinations and less on the ship as the entertainment. Though it is a smaller line, with only two ships, Clipper has twenty-two itineraries. The company manages to do this by implementing a very simple plan: go south in the winter and north in the summer. Voyages range in length from six to fifteen days, encompassing destinations along the coastal waterways of North America. On the Pacific coast, the ships cruise from Alaska to Costa Rica; on the eastern seaboard, they cruise from Prince Edward Island to Florida. They sail as far inland as the Great Lakes. They visit the Panama Canal, the British and U.S. Virgin Islands, the lower Caribbean and Orinoco River, the Grenadines, and the Windward and Leeward Islands.

These different destinations keep things interesting for everyone. Passengers keep coming back because there is always something new to do. Many people go on the Virgin Islands cruise more than once, because they find it to be a relaxing and wonderful cruise. Even there, however, the Clipper ships don't go to the big ports.

Aside from the Caribbean, Clipper's most popular destinations are Alaska and the antebellum South. It started offering a Great Lakes cruise this year, which sold out before the company could even publish an advertising brochure.

Alaska is always a popular destination. The cruise sells out quickly, so the wise customer will want to book early. Six months before the sailing date is not too soon.

ACCOMMODATIONS FOR SINGLES

On a Clipper cruise, it doesn't matter whether you're traveling alone or with a companion. It's purely a matter of personal preference. Singles who have traveled with the line say they felt comfortable traveling alone, because the crew took such good care of all of the passengers.

At no time is a single faced with going ashore alone. According to McQuinn, "If we go to a place, particularly where there is no infrastructure, the naturalists that travel on board will lead hikes ashore."

The line does try to pair up people who are looking for roommates. The single supplement is 1.5 times the cabin category rate. Advertised in the brochures is the category two rate. There are a limited number of singles in other categories. It depends on itinerary. The best thing is to talk to Clipper's reservations people and see what they can do. Occasionally they can offer a discount to a new client, but that is not something that is advertised. You also can inquire at a travel agency, but whatever information the agents have will be something they have received from Clipper.

The line occasionally offers discounts to groups, such as the Smithsonian or National Geographic Society.

PASSENGER INFORMATION

Since the Clipper line doesn't offer bingo, gambling, or the other types of onboard entertainment that the other lines provide, its ships tend to attract older, more sophisticated singles, people in their forties and fifties who are interested in the history, culture, and geography of places off the beaten path.

All sorts of people go on these cruises, however, because each cruise offers something for every personality. There are activities at all levels of energy. "I just got back from a ship yesterday," reports McQuinn, "and there was an eighty-five-year-old woman traveling alone. And this was by no means her first trip with us. I think that even if you're older, as long as you're healthy, there is no problem with anyone traveling alone."

ONBOARD LIFE

The onboard lifestyle is casual and unregimented, with none of the activities that typify the atmosphere on conventional cruise ships. There are no casinos, no discos, no lounge acts. Passengers can be as relaxed as they wish. Basically, your day will consist of getting to the destination and participating in the shore excursions.

The Clipper travel experience is enhanced by the presence of historians, naturalists, and other experts who bring the destinations to life in informal talks during shore excursions and over cocktails at the end of the day.

There is a single seating for dinner, and it's all unassigned. Naturally, the people aboard tend to get to know each other. "It's like being in a giant social gathering for a week," says McQuinn. On some of the big cruise lines, a single must make a dining room reservation; that's not the case here. Nothing formal is arranged. However, if the dining room manager notices that someone is having a hard time finding a place to sit, he or she will direct the person to a table and even make introductions. But people get to know each other very quickly. McQuinn says, "I've never heard that somebody is on the ship alone and is not happy because no one is talking to him or her." You can choose to sit with the same people or with different people at every meal.

Meals are always offered on board, but if you choose to skip one, that too is your prerogative. Often the ships overnight in places where passengers can eat ashore. On certain cruises, the dining staff holds a barbecue on shore. Many cruises offer occasions for which the chefs pack box lunches as part of a shore excursion.

Clipper's chefs come from the Culinary Institute of America. They use fresh meats, produce, and fish. They try to vary the dishes according to the region the ships are visiting by offering a sampling of the local cuisine. Basically, however, they offer wholesome American food. There are always two meat entrees, a pasta entree, and a vegetarian entree. You can get half portions, two half portions if you can't make up your mind, or even a portion and a half if you happen to be especially hungry. The cooking staff is happy to work with anyone on a special diet. If you have a favorite food that you simply must have on board, then let the cruise line know ahead of time and the staff will try to provide it.

Clipper recommends casual and comfortable dress on board: slacks and knits. Onshore dress is just as casual, because you will probably be going on hikes, walks, and explorations. In the evening, passengers usually don pantsuits and so forth. This is by no means a jacket-and-tie, formal-dress affair. There are two occasions on each trip—the captain's welcome aboard and farewell parties and dinners—for which people do tend to get a little more dressed up. Men will put on a jacket and tie, and women will wear nicer pantsuits, cocktail dresses, or even ethnic clothing picked up in the region. This is all based on personal preference, however. No rules are enforced. "I just want to stress, though, that there's never an occasion when you would need a tuxedo," says McQuinn.

The line shows a movie every night. On certain nights, hired entertainment comes on board, perhaps a steel band. In such a case, a cocktail party is held on board or the ship might announce a "pirate's night." There are no set arrangements that are followed on every cruise, although entertainers are almost always invited aboard.

The ships are equipped with nice observation lounges with a bar and a small library. Passengers congregate there to chat, play cards, and have drinks.

ITINERARY AND SEA SIGHTS

The ships' eight-foot drafts enable the small vessels to get very close to shorelines and explore secluded waterways not accessible to bigger ships.

The ships try to make a stop every day, but such stops depend on the itinerary. Also, it depends on what one means by a "stop." Some itineraries call for anchoring off an island to go ashore. There may not be a port, but the ships are stopping.

The line tries to leave a good portion of the day for the destination, unless there's a reason to cruise during the day. During a cruise of the antebellum South, for instance, people want to be on the water during the day because they want to see the passing scenery. It's the same for the Orinoco River, Panama Canal, or St. Lawrence Seaway cruises.

SHORE EXCURSIONS

Motorized, inflatable landing craft extend the travelers' reach into remote areas where no infrastructure exists. Passengers travel in small numbers in an intimate and congenial shipboard environment where everyone gets to meet each other. In the Sea of Cortez, Clipper offers a river cruise, which provides opportunities to hike and also to visit cities such as Trinidad.

The line offers hundreds of shore excursions. A single person is welcome to participate in any of them. Hikes are offered on levels that range from moderate to strenuous. If you want to just take a stroll through the woods, you could choose to do so. Walks and hikes are led by the ships' naturalists. As for the organized bus tours, none are strenuous, though some are rather long.

There are certain shore excursions that the elderly probably wouldn't join, like the rafting trip offered in Alaska. Or, if for example you know from experience that your back will hurt if you sit on a bus for seven or eight hours, then you will probably not want to do the Pacific Northwest overland and overnight excursion. It's a seven- to eight-hour stint on a bus followed by hikes. Passengers need to realize their limitations. The line gives a lot of information beforehand, and each traveler must decide what his or her physical ability and strength can bear.

The ships' naturalists can escort you around the natural environment, or the historians can guide you around the places of notable interest, all at no extra charge. Clipper offers more routine excursions, such as bus trips that feature, for instance, the history of a city. These are offered at an additional cost. Of course, you are welcome to explore on your own, at your own pace, if you so choose. The staff will give you whatever information you want. Just ask the cruise director.

THEME AND SPECIAL-INTEREST CRUISES

Clipper has some cruises that could be categorized as theme cruises. One cruise offers golfing along the Golden Strand, for instance. However, all Clipper cruises are theme cruises, in a way. The whole line is defined by the destination rather than by any events provided on board the ships. This goes back to the fact that the focus is on the destination and not what's on board.

CRUISING SEASONS

Clipper's ships are fully booked at all times of the year. There is no particular high or low season. Christmas or Easter, summer or fall, the line has been unable to track any particular time that is more popular with certain groups.

TIPPING

Tipping is entirely up to the passenger. When asked, Clipper suggests $9 a day per passenger. That amount will cover the entire crew. Officers do not get tipped, nor do the naturalists and historians. They are not included in the tip pool.

Tipping is handled at the end of the cruise. This is not a situation where you are constantly tipping a hotel bellboy. Clipper provides a box where tips can be placed. You can do it anonymously, or you can choose to write a check. So for a single person on a seven-day cruise, Clipper suggests you tip $63.

McQuinn reports, "I just met a couple on one of our cruises who had such a wonderful time that they thought nine dollars a day was a very modest tip. They tipped more than that, because they were so delighted with the service. I can honestly say I think there are very few who have sailed with us that do not feel that way. We're special!"

PRECRUISE INFORMATION

Clipper will send, with your ticket, a passenger information booklet that details the day-by-day itinerary, shore excursions, and travel information for the cruise. You'll learn what to pack, what the ship will be like, and so on. Also included is a suggested reading list so you can anticipate and enjoy your cruise even more. This handy information is put together in a little booklet that passengers receive thirty days prior to sailing.

CHAPTER 6

$\mathscr{C}$osta
Cruises

80 S.W. Eighth Street
Miami, FL 33130
Telephone (305) 358-7325 or (800) 462-6782

Costa Cruises is Europe's leading cruise line, with a modern fleet of ships and worldwide itineraries. Costa's international family of ships spans the globe. "We consider our line the leader in European cruising," says Linda Parrotta, vice president of marketing for Costa Cruises.

$\mathscr{G}$ENERAL SHIP INFORMATION

Costa's ships have a distinct Italian personality. The *Costa Victoria* is a new ship, and it is the cruise line's flagship. It weighs 75,000 tons and holds 1,950 passengers. The spectacular 1,350-passenger, 54,000-ton *CostaRomantica* joined the fleet in November 1993. The line has six ships all together: the *Costa Victoria*, the *CostaRomantica*, the *CostaAllegra*, the *CostaClassica*, the *CostaMarina*, and the *CostaRiviera*.

As a ship for singles, Parrotta recommends the *Costa Allegra*. It is one of the line's smaller, more intimate ships, holding 800 passengers.

$\mathcal{D}$ESTINATIONS, LENGTH OF CRUISES, DEPARTURE PORTS

Passengers can enjoy a European cruise on a Costa liner in the summer or a Caribbean cruise in the fall and winter. Passengers find the Caribbean a more relaxing vacation. A lot of older people cruise there just to relax and vacation; sometimes they bring their families. Europe is a more intense vacation—it is less relaxing and more on the go, with lots to see and lots to do.

The cruise line offers cruises of seven days and longer through the Caribbean, the Mediterranean, northern Europe, South America, and transatlantic. In winter (from October to April), the *Costa Victoria* and the *Costa Romantica* sail the Caribbean. The *Costa Victoria* sails to the western and eastern Caribbean, alternating every Sunday.

In the summer, all of Costa's ships go to Europe. Being the number one cruise line in Europe, the company has found it beneficial to deploy all its vessels to Europe for the high season there. The ships will be in Europe for the summer season, which stretches from May through October.

Sailing from the ports of Genoa, Venice, Amsterdam, and Copenhagen, Costa's vessels sail on seven-, ten-, eleven-, twelve-, and thirteen-night cruises to the eastern and western Mediterranean, the Canary Islands, the Baltic and Russia, the fjords, and the North Cape. The *Costa Victoria* takes seven-night eastern Mediterranean cruises, from Venice to Greece and Turkey, beginning May 4 through October 26, through 1998. During the same time periods, the *CostaRomantica* sails seven-night western Mediterranean cruises from Genoa to Italy, Tunisia, Spain, and France.

European cruises are generally seven to fourteen nights in length. Costa offers shorter cruises when it repositions a ship. For instance, it might offer a sailing from Venice to Genoa in midseason, which would be a five-night cruise. The repositioning cruises are listed in the Costa brochure. They are called Unique Voyages because you can get a little taste of sailing in Europe. The line offers over eighty seven-night cruise choices in Europe. The balance of the cruises range from seven to fourteen nights.

The Mediterranean is a very popular choice for Americans and Europeans alike.

ACCOMMODATIONS FOR SINGLES

"We do not specifically target singles, as certain cruise lines do," says Parrotta. "We don't think single women or men, especially financially secure women or men who are perhaps a bit older expect to go on a cruise and meet the love of their life. They want to have a nice time." Costa does have a lot of single cruisers, but they don't necessarily travel alone.

There are single supplements on Costa's European cruises, but single accommodations are available on all cruises on a request basis. They have a published rate, as indicated in the published material. For the new Caribbean season, Costa is offering a singles share program. The cruise line will do its best to match you with a same-sex single passenger so you can sail with a companion. "Of course, we cannot guarantee compatibility," says Parrotta. "I can't say that everything is going to be a perfect match." Still, you won't have to pay any additional supplements. You can book Costa's singles share program through your travel agent.

ᏇASSENGER INFORMATION

Costa has a large mix of passengers of different ages. In Europe, about 80 percent of passengers will be European. With the line's European ambience, taking a Costa cruise therefore is an adventure that differs distinctly from sailing with an all-American passenger list. This presents the opportunity for an experience that is slightly different for the typical North American.

The line promotes to cruisers thirty-five years old and up. The average first-time cruiser is about forty-seven years old, and the overall average is fifty-two years of age. "I wouldn't say our passengers are as old as on some of the other cruise lines, but I would say we have a very good mix, because we have both older and some that are younger," says Parrotta. "I think an older, single person would be very comfortable on our cruises."

ᏅNBOARD LIFE

Parrotta emphasizes that Costa is not a specifically singles-oriented cruise line. It cannot guarantee that many singles will be aboard. Neither does it offer a male dance host program. But you can still have a very good time if you're cruising alone on a Costa ship, because the atmosphere is so festive and friendly that you will likely meet people from all over the world.

When you board ship for a Costa Caribbean cruise, you are escorted to your stateroom by a white-gloved attendant, who shows you around and makes sure you are comfortable. In your cabin, you receive more information about the cruises, the programs, and what is happening for the day and for the night. You will also find information on shore excursions, which you should read about and book as soon as possible.

The first day, after boarding is complete, there is a Sail Away party. The entire cruise staff attends. It's festive and fun, with drink specials, snacks, and music. It really gets you into the spirit. All the bartenders are very friendly. If you take a seat at the pool bar, you will definitely be drawn into conversation.

The food on Costa ships is Italian in flavor and is offered with professional service. You can eat as much as you want. The kitchens offer meals all day long: buffets, afternoon teas, authentic Italian pizzas. Each night they feature a dinner specialty from a different region of Italy. There is always one Italian regional specialty on the menu. Of course, there is pasta at every lunch and dinner, but a wide selection of other choices is available as well, so the menu isn't exclusively Italian. There will be continental European cuisine as well.

Singles can tell the maitre d' that they would like to sit at a large table. The largest table seats ten. When the seating is arranged, single people usually end up at the same table anyway. Otherwise, seating is grouped before the ship sails, so you can make arrangements through your travel agent. Whatever your needs are, tell your travel agent about them. The more information Costa receives about you, the better for you.

If you like excitement, Costa has some pretty wacky theme nights. One is Festa Italiana, which is an Italian street festival at sea. On board is bocci ball, pizza dough tossing, and samplings of food from different areas of Italy. There is Venetian mask making as well. Soon the whole ship becomes a little Italian piazza, with many different activities going on.

Another night is the Captain's Night. This is a formal-dress evening in which the ship's captain greets all the guests. You can have your photo taken with the captain.

One theme night was voted one of the wackiest theme nights in the cruise industry by *Fielding World Wide Guide*. The event was Costa's Roman Bocano night, held on the last night of a cruise. It's a toga party.

BEST BETS FOR MEETING PEOPLE

If you feel you might need help meeting others, introduce yourself to the guest relations manager at the information desk on board the ship. That way, when others introduce themselves to the manager as single persons traveling alone, the manager can put you together.

Also, be sure to mention that you would like to sit at a large table for dinner.

SHORE EXCURSIONS

Tours are very popular in the Caribbean, and you should book early to make sure you get what you want. Some are offered on a limited basis due to limited space. Usually everyone who wants to take a tour gets the opportunity, but you shouldn't chance the possibility of being disappointed.

SPECIAL PACKAGES AND ADD-ONS

Costa feels that its shorter Unique Voyages are perfect for those who don't want a long cruise. With precruise and postcruise packages, they make a great vacation. Say you want to go to Venice for a couple of days and then take a five-day cruise over to Genoa and have a two-day postcruise package there. A Unique Voyage would be just the ticket.

There is one other type of cruise that singles in particular may like. For the second year in a row, Perillo Tours and Costa have joined forces to provide North Americans with the best of both worlds in European travel. You can now have a combined six-night escorted land package to the best of Italy and a seven-night cruise on the *CostaClassica* to the alluring Greek islands.

$\mathcal{P}$RECRUISE INFORMATION

Costa offers ninety-day early booking discounts. This is an opportunity for good pricing.

$\mathcal{N}$EW AND FUTURE POSSIBILITIES

Costa is considering other programs that lean toward single passengers. These new opportunities have not yet been developed, but customers should ask about them when booking.

CHAPTER 7

$\mathscr{C}$unard

555 Fifth Avenue
New York, NY 10017
Telephone (800) 728-6273
On-line address: http://www.cunardline.com

Cunard is the world's leading luxury cruise line. "Cunard operates the largest fleet of five-star-plus luxury ships in the world," says Eileen Daily, public relations manager for the line.

$\mathscr{G}$ENERAL SHIP INFORMATION

Cunard maintains a fleet of five elegant ships: the five-star-plus *Royal Viking Sun*, the five-star *Vistafjord*, the superyachts *Sea Goddess I* and *Sea Goddess II*, and the legendary *Queen Elizabeth 2 (QE2)*. The company's recent history has been one of growth through refurbishment. For example, the *QE2* underwent a $45 million overhaul and the *Vistafjord* had a $15 million dollar repair. The *Royal Viking Sun* and the two *Sea Goddess* ships received a combined total of $14.7 million in upgrading.

The two *Sea Goddess* superyachts are each 334 feet in length, and each holds 116 passengers. They have pioneered the idea of superyacht cruising to serve sophisticated passengers, re-creating the style, comfort, and luxury to which the most cos-mopolitan and cultivated travelers are accustomed. The *Sea Goddess* ships re-create an atmosphere of club life, featuring the utmost in personalized service, superyacht luxury, and exclu-sive destinations.

DESTINATIONS, LENGTH OF CRUISES, DEPARTURE PORTS

The ships call at more than 300 ports throughout the world.

Being smaller, the *Sea Goddess* yachts can sail to hideaways inaccessible to larger ships, allowing guests to discover primi-tive Spanish villages, little-known beaches, and exotic ports familiar only to elite international jet setters. Some favorite *Sea Goddess* ports of call include the picturesque Italian town of Portofina, the chic French island of Porquerolles, and historic Patmos, the most northerly of the Dodecanese Islands. *Sea Goddess I* and *II* sail the Mediterranean, the Orient, and the Caribbean. The Mediterranean is a very hot destination right now with all ages. The Caribbean is always popular as well. Cunard also offers voyages to Africa and Asia for the single seek-ing adventure.

Cunard travels all over the world. Some of the more unusual and exciting ports the ships visit are Mahe, the chief island of the Seychelles in the Indian Ocean; Istanbul; Singapore; Komodo Island in Indonesia; Haifa, Israel; and Reykjavik, Iceland. "We also have amazing cruises around the Greek islands, the Mediter-ranean, the Orient, and the Caribbean," says Daily. For something different and exciting, Cunard offers cruises around South America and around Scotland.

*A*CCOMMODATIONS FOR SINGLES

If you sail on the *Sea Goddess I* or *II*, you will have access to some of the most luxurious accommodations afloat. You will enjoy a spacious suite of rooms featuring large windows, a bedroom and separate sitting area, and a full bath. Other amenities include a safe, a video player, a complimentary stocked bar and refrigerator, and a telephone with worldwide direct dial.

*P*ASSENGER INFORMATION

Cunard's ships attract a variety of passengers, most of whom are affluent. Around 35 percent of the passengers on the *Royal Viking Sun* are older singles. The *Vistafjord* gets around 29 percent. Around 23 percent of passengers on the *Queen Elizabeth 2* are older singles; they are, however, somewhat younger than those who sail on the *Vistafjord* and the *Royal Viking Sun*. Cunard does not have any research on the two *Sea Goddess* ships, but they tend to attract a younger crowd.

More single men travel on the longer cruises and world cruises. These men have reached their peak financially and yet are very stimulated culturally in terms of learning about new places and traveling. Cunard has two world cruises every year, on the *QE2* and the *Royal Viking Sun*. "We have many single men on these cruises," says Daily.

*O*NBOARD LIFE

Sea Goddess life is most remarkable for what it lacks—regimented activities, assigned seating, deck sports, even gratuities. A European and American staff of eighty-nine people caters to every whim of the select 116 *Sea Goddess* guests. To help ensure outstanding service, a personal preference form is mailed to all guests before their cruise, requesting information about favorite beverages, foods, and activities. Guests may indulge in Beluga caviar at any time. They may even have it served to them while they are resting in a Jacuzzi. They may enjoy a picnic lunch, complete with French champagne in a silver bucket, on a deserted island. Or perhaps they fancy a specially chartered flight to spectacular sights ashore. *Sea Goddess* passengers can request a four- or five-course meal twenty-four hours a day. A full bar, with selections made by passengers on their personal preference form, is set up in each cabin. In addition, complimentary wines, spirits, champagne, and caviar are served throughout the cruise.

Offering the freedom of a private yacht is the key to the *Sea Goddess* concept. Guests can dine when they wish, sit where they want, and linger as long as they like in the ship's dining salon, which *Travel and Leisure* magazine compared to a two-star Michelin restaurant.

There are no seating arrangements on either the *Sea Goddess I* or *Sea Goddess II*. There is one main dining salon. However, passengers can dine at the outdoor cafe for breakfast or lunch for an informal setting.

The "big" ships also offer alternative and less formal dining areas for those who do not want to dress for breakfast and lunch. Eating on the deck or in the dining room is a matter of personal preference. The Lido Cafe on the *QE2* provides an informal dining experience for breakfast, lunch, afternoon tea, and the midnight buffet.

For those sailing on the *QE2*, arrangements in the formal dining room are made according to cabin level. Single seating is available. As for the *Royal Viking Sun* and the *Vistafjord*, passengers should request how many people they would like to have at their table when they book the cruise.

There is only one main dining room on the *Royal Viking Sun*, and it has single seating. On this ship there is an alternative restaurant called Venezia. You may make a reservation once on board, usually once a voyage. The Garden Cafe provides an informal dining experience for breakfast and lunch.

On the *Vistafjord* is one main dining room, which is single seating. The Lido Cafe provides an informal dining experience for breakfast and lunch.

Many activities are offered on the big ships. It is said that it would take a person four months to participate in all the activities on the *QE2*. On a *Sea Goddess* yacht, one can even go jet skiing off the diving platform. All the ships offer fitness and spa facilities.

On the *Royal Viking Sun*, the Stella Polaris Room, with its 300-degree ocean view, is perfect for enjoying a cocktail or an espresso. The Norway Lounge presents Broadway-style shows and revues at night. The Compass Rose Room and Oak Room are good for quiet moments.

*B*EST BETS FOR MEETING PEOPLE

Cunard's ships each vary as to places for singles to congregate. The *QE2* has a variety of bars and lounges. The Crystal Bar is good for predinner and postdinner drinks. The Golden Lion Pub is an informal British bar. The Chart Room is an elegant bar with a piano that once graced Cunard's *Queen Mary*. The Yacht Club is a bar and lounge by day, a cabaret and nightclub by night. The casinos are also a popular place to meet people. Cunard has casinos on all five ships.

On the *Royal Viking Sun*, the Midnight Sun Lounge is a lively gathering place. Activities take place here during the day, and there is dancing during the cocktail hour and late-night disco. The Norway Lounge also offers dancing in the evening.

Club Viking, on the *Vistafjord*, is an exciting cabaret and nightclub. The North Cape Bar, however, is *the* favorite gathering place for passengers. It's great for cocktails and conversation.

Since the *Sea Goddess* yachts are small, the best places for singles to congregate are the main salon, at the piano bar in the club salon, and on the sundeck.

Single passengers who want to make the most of their trip are advised to be as social as possible. They should participate in activities on the ship as well as on shore. Longer cruises and very exciting cruises seem to draw people out. If you are single, you can probably find a friend to travel with you as far as Florida or the Caribbean, but how easy is it to get a friend to go with you on a two- or three-month cruise? As a result, these cruises tend to have more passengers who are alone.

"You'll make friends, believe me," says Daily. "At Cunard, we find that what draws one single to another is a strong sense of self, a traveler who wants to do things for himself or herself to enrich the mind and one's health. Cruising is a great way for such individuals."

SHORE EXCURSIONS

When one of the *Sea Goddess* yachts is in port, Cunard arranges access to some of the world's most elite private golf and tennis resorts, private nightclubs, and private beaches.

CRUISING SEASONS

Cunard has no research on the best time of the year for singles to cruise, but many people like to travel in the warmer months, so the spring and summer are very popular. Singles sail year-round.

$\mathcal{H}$olland America Line

300 Elliot Avenue West
Seattle, WA 98119
Telephone (800) 426-0327

The Holland America Line marked its 124th year in business in 1997, making it one of the oldest cruise lines around. "We are known for our experience, outstanding crews, service, and excellent food," says William Pedlar, vice president of marketing. The ships are impeccable, and the award-winning line consistently maintains its level of grandeur. The line has carried more than seven million passengers.

$\mathcal{G}$ENERAL SHIP INFORMATION

Holland America's five-star fleet includes the 1,214 passenger MS *Nieuw Amsterdam*, its sister ships MS *Noordam*, the 1,494 passenger MS *Westerdam*, and the new 1,266 passenger sister ships ms *Statendam*, MS *Maasdam*, MS *Ryndam*, and MS *Veendam*. The 62,000-gross-ton 1,320 passenger *Rotterdam* VI (the original *Rotterdam* was retired on September 30, 1997) is scheduled for delivery in October 1997. Two additional 65,000-gross-ton, 1,440-passenger ships are under construction in Italy and scheduled for delivery in 1999. Holland America Line is today the second most profitable cruise line in the world, and the success they say has been the phenomenal passenger response to their Statendam-class ships. These ships bring together old world elegance that their repeat cruisers seem to enjoy so much. Yet all have state-of-the-art technology. Cabins are much larger than many other ships of the same category.

DESTINATIONS, LENGTH OF CRUISES, DEPARTURE PORTS

Holland America ships sail to the Caribbean and Panama Canal year-round and seasonally to Alaska, Europe, and New England. They make transatlantic cruises in the summer. In the spring and fall, they sail to Hawaii. The line is also known for its world cruises.

PASSENGER INFORMATION

The median age of Holland America passengers varies, depending on the length of the cruise, but in general the line attracts older singles in their forties, fifties, and sixties. Younger singles tend to go for the shorter cruises and the Caribbean-type cruises. Older singles travel to the Mediterranean and to Alaska and in general take longer cruises, primarily because they have the time.

"Whether singles are better off traveling by themselves or with another single friend depends entirely on the person," says Pedlar. "I think it depends on each passenger's circumstances and degree of confidence." About 15 percent of Holland

America's total passengers are single women. The majority travel with other women, but a fair number of women travel alone.

More women travel on Holland America cruises than do men. In the older age groups, women make up a larger percentage of the population. You may see widows traveling with other women. This is reflective of the population mix. There simply are more women in their fifties and sixties than there are men. Most of those who enjoy cruising want to meet other people, not necessarily to find romance.

Also, as much as cruise lines would like to change this, women are more receptive to the things a cruise provides. They are very interested in a cruise-type of vacation, particularly the pampering of not having to make the bed, cook dinner, wash the dishes, or do laundry. Women enjoy the pure pleasure of having someone else take care of them for a change. They also appreciate the safety.

ONBOARD LIFE

Holland America cruises usually have at least two formal nights, depending upon the length of the cruise. On a 13-day cruise you might have two or more. There are always your informal nights, but "elegantly casual" seems to be more the order of the day. On longer cruises you will find older passengers, and they tend to be more formal in their dress. You will see more suits and ties, and more of a "dress" look rather than an informal one. The "elegantly casual" look seems to blend in with Holland America's old world charm and elegance that you find throughout their ships.

The first thing a passenger can do upon boarding the ship is study the daily activity sheet, *Dagelyks Nieuws* (daily news). You'll find many activities of interest, from facials, saunas, and massages to aerobics and sporting tournaments.

Before dinner, Holland America holds a cocktail hour featuring complimentary hot and cold hors d'oeuvres in the main lounge. A majority of the passengers will attend, so this is a good opportunity to socialize and relax. Again, the *Dagelyks Nieuws*, which is delivered to every cabin each evening, will be the passenger's best friend. It will note when and what is happening.

On all ships, the dining room is divided into a first, or early, seating and a second, or main, seating. Although there are usually not a lot of children on Holland America cruises, generally families will choose the first seating. "I think the way to approach dinner is for people to ask themselves if they are morning people," says Pedlar. "If you are the type who likes to get up at five or six o'clock in the morning and take a walk around the promenade deck as the sun is rising, then you will probably prefer the first seating. If you are the type who likes to stay up past midnight and you don't really care if you eat breakfast or only want a croissant or room service, then you'll probably be better off with the second seating."

Table arrangements are on a request basis. Singles can request a table for two, four, six, or eight. When you go into the dining room for breakfast or lunch, the stewards or maitre d' will ask whether you would like to sit with other people or you prefer a table by yourself. If you want to sit with other people, the steward will escort you and introduce you to your dining mates. If you like them, you will be sure to see them in the bars and lounges and at the shows and activities throughout the rest of the cruise. If you don't like them, you really never have to socialize with them again.

In some cases, on the second or third night of sailing, people do request a change of tables. If you wish, you can ask the maitre d' to move you to another table, but depending on how full the ship is, your request may or may not be fulfilled. Usually there is some degree of flexibility, however, and the move will probably not be a problem.

After dinner, people break up to find their favorite brands of entertainment. Some will go to the casino. "That is of surprisingly high interest to people over fifty," says Pedlar. "I'm not sure why, but demographically we've seen that on a national basis the interest in gambling is increasing dramatically." Others will go to the piano bar, which is more intimate, where they can sing along to the old tunes. Some will go to the main lounge (each ship has a different name for its main lounge), where there will be dance music. On certain nights, the entertainment in the lounges is themed; for instance, they may have a country and western night. The majority of people will go to the show lounge, where the main entertainment is staged each evening.

The ships do not have singles lounges per se. Choices are a matter of interest and style. Almost every cruise ship does have a disco, called the Crow's Nest Lounge, so late in the evening that is probably where young and single people will congregate. The contemporary music played there most evenings will attract the younger crowd.

Holland America has dance hosts on cruises of fourteen days or longer: its Panama Canal cruises, the Grand Voyages, and its Hawaii cruises. They are also available on a few of the longer holiday cruises, such as Christmas and New Year's cruises. These longer cruises generally attract an older clientele, the majority of whom are women. The social hosts are available for conversation, to provide the opportunity for single women to dance, to play bridge, and for simple companionship throughout the cruise. The ships employ them as facilitators, to bring people together.

Regardless of the availability of social hosts, the officers on board each ship will be in the lounges in the evening. They serve basically the same function. They are available for dancing and will visit at the tables to socialize. To some extent, all officers on board act as facilitators, as they might for a large party in their own home.

In keeping with the spirit and the ambience of the cruise ships, none of the activities are designed for couples only. Of course, couples are welcome to enjoy all activities on board the ship, as are singles, whether they are traveling with others or alone. Almost every activity is planned to feel more like an evening party in one's own home. It will be much like any other social gathering where singles and couples feel comfortable together.

Holland American offers lots of activities for early birds. Many passengers are out doing their five laps around the promenade deck at 6:00 A.M., just for the air. This seems to be especially popular among singles in their fifties. There are aerobic classes and jazzercise classes and all levels of activities for those who start early. On the other hand, those who stayed up late the night before may prefer to rise later and perhaps settle for nothing more active than a casual, light breakfast on the lido deck.

Sometime during the day, passengers will probably choose to lie in the sun for a while. They might even have lunch on deck. The fair-skinned may prefer to stay indoors in the afternoon and play bridge or backgammon. Many enjoy the late afternoon sun for reading a book on deck. Feel free to walk around the ship and find the one spot that looks right and feels right—perhaps the poolside or the promenade deck—and plant yourself (deck chairs cannot be reserved, however). From about 6:00 P.M. until midnight, there is probably an average of six to eight different activities at any given time.

The only thing the line charges for are massages, facials, or services in the beauty salon, as is common with all cruise lines.

Holland America has some of the best spas at sea. Says Pedlar, "The spas are beautifully laid out facilities, with lovely views and lots of aerobic machines." The ships have male and female personal trainers to help passengers get the most out of the spa. The personal trainers will design exercise programs and show you how to use the machines. If you already have an exercise program, the trainers can translate it into the machines available on the ship.

Holland America has spa cuisine as well, which is lighter and healthier. "Calling it 'light' does it a disservice," says Pedlar. The foods are fat reduced, salt reduced, and cholesterol reduced, with at least three choices on every menu. The menu will specifically list the sodium, fat, and cholesterol levels. "We have the largest, most extensive menus on any cruise ship," Pedlar continues. "On every single menu—breakfast, lunch, and dinner—items will be identified with a heart symbol, showing it as the light and healthy choice."

The Holland America outdoor and casual dining has been rated the best at sea. "It is being copied by everybody now," says Pedlar. "We have been doing it for so long that it's hard to remember when we didn't do it."

The hostess and the cruise director on board each ship are extremely valuable resources for specific recommendations about activities or shore excursions. The cruise director and the cruise staff in general are valuable assets to the single passenger. There are many programs going on simultaneously, and the staff will review each day's activities. They may notice, for example, that a lot of single people came to play bridge. This makes them particularly aware of the needs of the singles on board.

In addition, singles should feel free to speak to the cruise director about their needs. Staff members will be extremely responsive in making suggestions for activities and even in making introductions. "They really treat people's onboard experience as if they were having a party in their home," says Pedlar. "The officers and the hostess and the cruise director—this is their party, and they want to do everything they can for their guests, to make sure that they are having a good time. So they will make introductions and make suggestions, or they will simply sit and enjoy the company."

You will have no trouble finding staff; they are identifiable by their uniforms or blazers. In fact, the entire staff, from the captain of the ship to the onboard physician, is introduced the first evening, after dinner in the main lounge. The line will also post each staff member's picture, so that even before you start walking around the ship you can view what is jokingly called the "Wanted Board."

*B*EST BETS FOR MEETING PEOPLE

Generally, singles traveling alone or with other singles should opt for a larger table for six or eight, so they have more people to meet. If you tell the maitre d' that you would like to be placed with other single people, the maitre d' will certainly try to honor that request. "My personal experience is that singles traveling together mix extremely well and enjoy the company because of the general age group," says Pedlar. "They just fit right in, and everyone enjoys each other."

Another opportunity to meet people is during breakfast and lunch, which doesn't have as structured a seating plan as dinner. Only at night does the dining room staff split passengers into two formal seatings. At all other times, you can go into the dining room and sit where you would like, which leads to a mingling of passengers. Breakfast and lunch are also served on deck in the lido area. This offers an informal dining experience that allows people to mix and meet in a casual atmosphere.

"One other thing happens constantly on board the ships," says Pedlar. "From the very first dinner, people are asking each other, 'What are you doing tomorrow? When we arrive, which shore excursion are you going to take?' People are generally interested in what other people are doing, and you inevitably will find, in the natural course of conversations, people who are planning to do what you want to do. They naturally come together in the course of the excitement about upcoming activities and port calls."

Singles should consult their daily events sheets and find the activities that interest them. Inevitably, many people of similar age and similar interests will choose similar activities. You can always find people who want to do the same thing as you, which will help you link up with like-minded passengers.

The first night, you will probably socialize with your tablemates from dinner. "Unless, of course, they are so boring you don't want to see them again," jokes Pedlar. "In which case, everyone politely excuses themselves and disappears." What generally happens, though, is people start discussing their after-dinner plans. Inevitably, others are invited to come along. That's just the beginning. Day by day, activity by activity, you will meet more people.

The more you get involved, the more fun you will have. If you want to meet people, you have to join in the activities. Sometimes people traveling alone are shy and order breakfast in their room and so forth. This is a no-no. Go to the dining room. Get out of your cabin and do something you want to do. The Holland America staff will be glad to help. If you want to play bridge, the staff will find you a bridge partner. Many traveling singles play cards. Even in the case of a traveling couple, one might play bridge and the other might not. All sorts of people join in the various activities.

SHORE EXCURSIONS

Travelers should take the time to review all the options available in each port. There is always a port lecture and a shopping lecture the day before the ship arrives in a new port. These are repeated via videotape through the television systems in the cabins, so if you miss the live program, you can watch it in your stateroom at your convenience anytime during the evening or the following morning.

Singles can choose whatever excursion is of interest to them. If you want to go kayaking, then you should go kayaking, because other singles will also be doing it. Holland America tries to design experiences for any number of interests. If singles select excursions according to their interests, then they will automatically be thrown together with other people who have similar interests.

𝒫ERSONAL SAFETY

Today, people are very concerned about traveling alone and being safe. Cruising is far and away one of the safest vacations possible, from a variety of perspectives. For one thing, it is an all-inclusive vacation, which means a lot less hassle for you. It's also less intimidating, from the time you make your reservations with the travel agent to your flight to the cruise itself. All these arrangements and reservations are handled in one simple process. That in itself offers a kind of security and peace of mind.

In addition, on a cruise you will be with people of like ages and interests, which offers the safety of a shared point of view. People generally feel comfortable in a homogenous group. The cruise ship is a floating resort, taking everyone together to a variety of ports that have been preselected for safety. All the shore excursions have also been designed for quality. Another thing to consider is that this floating resort is a self-contained system, so there is never any worry about water, food preparation, or other such concerns. All Holland America ships conform to U.S. public health regulations. When compared to hotels in terms of water quality, food quality, and incidence of problems, the cruise ship will always come up the winner. A ship is much, much safer than any hotel, and that safety is guaranteed.

People always worry when traveling as singles what will happen if they get sick. If you are in a foreign country by yourself and you become sick or injured, it can be a real hassle—and very scary. If you are on a cruise and your tablemates don't see you for a day, somebody will check on you very quickly. A cabin attendant will be able to check on you. There is medical attention available all the time. When you are in the cruise environment, you know you have people looking out for you.

"The Holland America line, without any doubt, has the absolute highest standard within the cruise industry for our medical facilities," says Pedlar. Every ship and every cruise has a staff of doctors and nurses at all times. A well-equipped hospital is on board, with the most modern facilities possible.

If there is one thing you should probably not do as a single, it's venture out completely alone on shore excursions. There are a variety of formal shore excursions. If you don't want to take a planned shore excursion, the cruise line has arranged organized walks or transfers to beaches. This way, even though you are pretty much independent, you will still be near other passengers from the ship. If you want to go shopping, take the shopping tour to ensure guidance and safety.

Pedlar acknowledges that of Holland America's destinations, Alaska is relatively safe: "It's perfectly safe to walk around in the Alaska ports." To get the most out of Alaska, though, you should participate in the shore excursions.

THEME AND SPECIAL-INTEREST CRUISES

The line features special cruises of twelve, fourteen, and sixteen days in length over the Christmas and New Year's period.

Holland America also offers two cruises a year, called Grand Voyages. The winter Grand Voyage is a world cruise. The ship actually sails around the world, but that does not mean every passenger aboard has to buy the 100-day cruise. One of the beauties of the world cruises is that people can get on at any place and get off at any subsequent point. It provides the opportunity for a cruise from about ten days up to one hundred days.

In the fall, the other Grand Voyage is offered. It is different each year and is generally from thirty-five to sixty-five days in length. In 1996, the Grand Voyage was a cruise from Australia to New Zealand. In 1997, it is a South Pacific cruise. In 1998, it will sail around South America. The median age of passengers on a Grand Voyage is about sixty-eight years, and the age range of the dance hosts is sixties to seventies. Very few lines have anything like this. It's a program for which Holland America gets rave reviews.

𝒩EW AND FUTURE POSSIBILITIES

Holland America has two more ships on the way, increasing its fleet to ten. Also, it will soon have a new port for passengers. The line has purchased the uninhabited 2,400-acre Bahamian island of Little San Salvador. This private island is regarded by many Bahamians as the most beautiful island in the group. It is 100 miles southeast of Nassau, between southern Eleuthera and Cat Island.

Holland America plans to build what it will call Half Moon Cay on the island. It will feature an idyllic setting with a spectacular crescent-shaped, white sand beach more than a mile in length. It will front on a protected bay leading to Exuma South. The bay affords excellent snorkeling among beautiful coral heads.

Holland America will have a network of nature trails around the facility that will allow passengers to explore the natural setting of the island at their leisure during a day-long port call. There will be shops and even a chapel, which will be used for weddings and vow-renewal ceremonies.

Half Moon Cay will be a featured port call on the MS *Westerdam*'s new seven-day Four Ports Plus Eastern Caribbean itinerary, beginning in 1998.

$\mathcal{N}$orwegian Cruise Line

7665 Corporate Center Drive
Miami, FL 33136
Telephone (305) 436-0866 or (800) 327-7030

The Norwegian Cruise Line is known for its fabulous entertainment and its acclaimed sports and special-interest cruises. It is the official cruise line of the National Basketball Association and the National Football League's Players Association, and it is the only line authorized to televise live games and broadcasts on board. Three out of five of their modern superliners feature a sports bar and grill so that fans can have multiple television access.

$\mathcal{G}$ENERAL SHIP INFORMATION

Norwegian has eight superliners, including the 1,050-passenger *Norwegian Crown,* the 1,504-passenger *Seaward,* the 1,456-passenger *Dreamward* and the sister ship *Windward,* the 800-passenger *Dynasty,* the 848-passenger *Norwegian Star,* the 950-passenger *Leeward,* and the line's flagship, the SS *Norway,* which can hold over 2,000 passengers.

DESTINATIONS, LENGTH OF CRUISES, DEPARTURE PORTS

Norwegian sails to the Bahamas and the Caribbean year-round and the Panama Canal in May and September. From spring to fall, cruises take in Bermuda and Alaska.

The line has several other interesting itineraries. The *Norwegian Crown* offers a series of Mediterranean sailings. The *Seaward* offers alternating exotic Caribbean and Barbados sailings each Sunday, from San Juan. A popular run from New York to Bermuda is offered by the *Dreamward*. The SS *Norway* offers five seven-day cruises to the western Caribbean. The *Leeward* makes three- and four-day cruises from Miami to the Bahamas, Key West, and Mexico year-round.

Norwegian Alaska cruises have been selling out every season. The Caribbean is still the most popular destination, however. Fran Sevcik, director of public relations for Norwegian Cruise Lines, reports, "Bermuda is gorgeous, a very beautiful island, very safe, just a lovely place to be." If you are a beach person, the Caribbean is probably for you. If you are the type that likes archaeology, you may find the ruins and pyramids in Mexico interesting.

ACCOMMODATIONS FOR SINGLES

Norwegian offers a guaranteed singles rate that is published in its brochure. With the guaranteed singles rate, Norwegian picks the cabin. If you want to pick your own cabin, depending upon availability, you might have to pay 150 to 200 percent of the usual fare.

$\mathcal{P}$ASSENGER INFORMATION

The highest percentage of singles and the youngest age group of passengers are attracted to Norwegian's shorter cruises, such as the three-day cruises. Norwegian offers three- and four-day cruises year-round.

Norwegian books a wide age range of passengers, but the average passenger is thirty-five to fifty-five years old. There are quite a few singles both younger and older than that.

The most popular destination among younger singles, according to Norwegian's statistics, is the eastern Caribbean. For older singles, the most popular destination is Alaska. Sevcik reports, "I think traditionally Alaska has been the destination for older singles, although we are seeing median ages coming down for that area."

$\mathcal{O}$NBOARD LIFE

The first day, everyone should get acquainted with the ship. You'll find the day's activities listed in the *Cruise News* delivered to your cabin. Walk around and get familiar with everything: the different lounges, the facilities, the pools, the sundeck, and the health club. Three of Norwegian's superliners feature a sports bar and grill for fans. Whatever your interests, getting familiar with the ship is important. See if there are any shore excursions you want to take, because those book very quickly. "That's advice for singles and nonsingles," say Sevcik. "Review what kinds of shore excursions are offered and try to get signed up for those right away."

Singles might want to check out the pool first. Each ship has a different pool area catering to different tastes. You can't reserve chairs, however. It is first come, first served. Norwegian has pool attendants on all of its ships. This is a new service, in which a staff member is available to help you find a lounge chair or to move a chair for you—and give you a nice, fluffy towel to boot. Pool attendants also walk around and give the occasional spritz of ice-cold water to those who like it. "So if you are sunbathing," says Sevcik, "and you want to cool off, they will come by and give you a spritz."

Four Norwegian ships offer several small, intimate dining rooms. If you want to meet other people, the dining rooms are the place to do it. The ships have a variety of table sizes, so when you book, tell your travel agent what size you prefer. Your request is noted in the booking record. Once you are on board the ship, if you are not happy with the table arrangement, you should talk to the maitre d'. The maitre d' will then try to accommodate you. Sevcik warns, "If the ship is full or other circumstances intervene, then it is not always possible." The very best plan, however, is to make your preferences known while booking your cruise with your travel agent. If you don't, you will be assigned a table automatically. Let the travel agent know that you are single and would like to be put at a table with other singles, or if that's not possible, at a table with a large group—if that is your desire.

The *Dreamward* and the *Windward* have lounges called Lucky's. They are found near the casino and the main show lounge. It is a horseshoe-shaped lounge, making it somewhat intimate in setting. Usually a small combo or a solo pianist will be playing. On the *Seaward* is a lounge called Oscar's Piano Bar, which has sing-alongs. It's a fun place for singles.

Norwegian is known for its entertainment. Don't miss any of the shows. They are wonderful; afterwards, you'll find there is still plenty of time to enjoy more nightlife. "Have dinner, go to a show, and then go on from there," suggests Sevcik.

There is no assigned seating in the theater, but people tend to be so friendly on cruises that it should be easy to strike up a conversation with your neighbors. "I don't think solo travelers feel like they are alone on Norwegian's ships, because there are so many people around at all times," according to Sevcik. Spending time alone becomes just a matter of preference.

All the ships have fitness centers, and they offer aerobic activities, including classes and group walks. Other fitness activities include volleyball, basketball, and Ping-Pong. They are all informal. Passengers just show up and join in. There is an extra charge for spa services, but if you want a massage, a facial, or some type of therapy, it will be available. Many passengers enjoy the pampering of spa services. Passengers can sign up when they board or the day before they want the service. Be aware, however, that key times get taken up quickly, so it pays to sign up ahead of time. Key times are usually at-sea days. Most people don't use the spa when the ship is in port.

BEST BETS FOR MEETING PEOPLE

Singles do find each other on Norwegian's cruises. Usually on the first night there is a singles party on each of the line's ships. It will be listed in your *Cruise News*. It is held in one of the lounges or maybe even in the disco. All single passengers are encouraged to come, and the event is a great icebreaker. The staff creates a little bit of fun with games, allowing people to meet.

Some singles like to sit by the bar in the pool area, a common congregating place. The bars near the pools have television sets to play the sports broadcasts for which the line is noted. "It is a little gathering spot," says Sevcik. "If I were a single and that was my scene, I might check out that area to find conversation with other people."

However, Sevcik warns, "When you are a single, you hope that every vacation might be a romantic encounter. But I think the better idea is that you want to have a good time, and if you meet someone, that is a great plus."

Certain lounges, like Lucky's, are natural gathering spots. All the ships have evening discos, which are obviously places where people congregate. Strike up a conversation with other people and enter the room with them. It's very easy to get assimilated into a group if that is what you want to do.

The cruise staff is very open and friendly to the needs of singles who want to meet others, although they are not matchmakers. Still, if you really want some suggestions on activities to help in your personal quest, the entire cruise staff will be happy to give you some tips or try to help.

SHORE EXCURSIONS

Many different shore excursions are provided. The majority of them are planned for groups, so it doesn't matter if you are traveling alone or with other people. Usually, the excursions will include a busload or vanload of people, so you will be with others anyway. Possibilities include snorkeling, sightseeing, shopping, visiting ruins, and so on, according to your personal preference. None of them are solo activities.

The cruise directors give a port lecture, and the shore excursion manager talks about the different tours that are available. Norwegian strongly suggests you sign up as soon as you can for the shore excursions you prefer, because they do sell out quickly.

There is no guarantee that after the first day what you want will be still be available. If there is something really special you want to do, it's always wiser to sign up sooner rather than later.

The shore excursion lectures include information about shopping. There are certain shops in each port that have special promotions for Norwegian passengers. Naturally, these are recommended. Items purchased in these stores carry a limited guarantee. If something proves wrong with the merchandise, according to the agreement, the vendors will make good on the wares.

The prices in Norwegian's onboard stores are competitive with shopping in the ports of call. They have a good selection of merchandise but cannot carry the extensive stocks you will find ashore.

PERSONAL SAFETY

The safety of going off on your own depends on where you are, what island you are on, the destination, and the type of activity you plan to do. The cruise directors and shore excursion managers give passengers warnings about certain places that are not considered as safe as others. Sometimes when in a foreign place, you don't know exactly where you are and you don't know the customs, so you might look a little vulnerable. It is not a bad idea to be with other people or to stick with an escorted tour, especially if you are traveling solo. There is always safety in numbers.

"That is not to say that people can't safely plan their own excursion, or go shopping by themselves," says Sevcik. "It doesn't mean you have to have a bodyguard everywhere you go." Still, you should use the same common sense and judgment that you would use at home.

THEME AND SPECIAL-INTEREST CRUISES

Norwegian's theme cruises focus on interests ranging from country music to jazz and blues. One week each year, in the fall, the line features a Big Band cruise to the eastern Caribbean. Dance hosts are available on this cruise.

CRUISING SEASONS

Norwegian welcomes many families aboard its ships during holidays and in the summer. If single cruisers aren't looking for a voyage among families and children, they should avoid summer and the major holidays. These include Easter, spring break, Thanksgiving, Christmas, and the summer vacation season.

TIPPING

Tipping on a Norwegian ship is fairly uniform. Guidelines are provided. Of course, tipping is always optional, though most people do.

PRECRUISE INFORMATION

Norwegian recommends that passengers check the material and brochures that will be sent in advance of boarding to get a general idea of the ports their ship will visit and onshore activities. That information is provided so that passengers can determine which shore excursions they would like to sign up for once aboard the ship.

CHAPTER 10

*P*rincess Cruises

10100 Santa Monica Boulevard
Los Angeles, CA 90067
Telephone (310) 553-1770 or (800) LOVE-BOAT

Princess Cruises is one of the three largest cruise lines in the industry, according to Jill Biggins, manager of media relations at Princess Cruises. Princess has become a leader in the industry, offering a wide variety of sailings to the most exotic (and most numerous) destinations in the world. The company offers excellent food, spacious cabins, and glamorous ships, along with good value in pricing.

*G*ENERAL SHIP INFORMATION

Princess currently operates a fleet of seven ships. Included are the *Island Princess* and *Pacific Princess*, twin sister ships, which weigh 20,000 tons and hold 640 passengers each. Then you have the larger *Crown Princess* and *Regal Princess*, 70,000 tons each, that cruise with 1,590 passengers. The *Sun Princess* and *Dawn Princess*, another set of twins, hold 1,950 passengers at 77,000 tons.

Finally, there is the *Royal Princess,* which holds 1,200 passengers at 45,000 tons.

In May 1998 the grand dame of the world, the *Grand Princess*—Princess Cruises' most expensive and the world's largest ship (taking that title away from Carnival's *Destiny*), will make her debut. Measuring 109,000 tons and costing approximately $450 million, the Grand Princess is roughly four times the length of Grand Central Station in New York City. She is larger than many buildings and world landmarks—in fact, the original Love Boat, the *Pacific Princess,* could fit inside the *Grand Princess'* Horizon Court dining and lido area.

*D*ESTINATIONS, LENGTH OF CRUISES, DEPARTURE PORTS

Princess Cruises offers nearly 150 different itineraries with over 200 ports of call worldwide—more than any other major cruise line. The line's four main destinations are the Caribbean, Alaska, Europe, and the Panama Canal. For its Alaska cruises, Princess offers more itineraries, more ships, and more departure dates than does any other line.

*A*CCOMMODATIONS FOR SINGLES

The single person who wants to cruise but doesn't want to travel alone might want to take advantage of Princess's Single Share program, which will match up the single traveler with another single person of the same sex. The program tries to match travelers according to details such as age and smoking/nonsmoking preference. The single person then travels as a double-occupancy passenger, getting the double-occupancy rate. "Singles might think about something like this in terms of possibly making a new friend," says Biggins. You can make this type of reservation through your travel agent. If you don't want to participate in the Single Share program, you can have your own single cabin, however, it will be costly. The rate will be 150 percent of what you would pay for double occupancy.

$\mathcal{P}$ASSENGER INFORMATION

The Caribbean is the number one cruising destination for single passengers. Younger singles in particular like this warm-weather itinerary.

More exotic itineraries usually get the older singles, ranging in ages from their forties to their seventies. Many of these passengers like what is called the Exotic Adventures cruises, which take from twelve to sixteen days to sail anywhere from Asia to the South Pacific and South America. Older singles also like Princess's cruises to Europe during the spring and summer. These are aboard the smaller, 640-passenger ships.

Every cruise is different. One cruise might have more single men, and another might have more single women. Younger singles might take a holiday cruise at Christmas or Easter. For older single men or women, the season is immaterial—it's the destination that counts with them.

$\mathcal{O}$NBOARD LIFE

The first seating for dinner is usually at 6:00 P.M. If for whatever reason you don't like your table, see the maitre d' as soon as possible. Nine times out of ten, the maitre d' will be able to do something. If you are with a group or are traveling as a couple, it may be harder to move you. Whatever your situation, though, it's always best to talk with the maitre d' as soon as possible.

The dining room typically has open seating at lunch, so you are able to sit with different people. Also, on the bigger ships, you have the option of eating lunch in the pizzeria or from the buffet on deck rather than in the dining room.

Princess offers a multitude of activities on every one of its cruises. Activities are not for everyone, however. Some passengers just want to stretch out on a deck chair and read, which is also fine.

Passengers enjoy Princess's evening entertainment. After dinner, you might want to attend one of these shows with people from your table. Or you might choose to go to the piano bar, the disco, the casino, or any one of Princess's lounges. Walk around and see what looks interesting to you. The larger ships have a piano bar with sing-alongs. There are also a lot of activities for which you can assemble a team and participate.

The Caribbean cruises offer pool games and usually live music in the pool areas. It's definitely a party environment there. A few of the ships also have a pool bar.

Princess has a program called Cruisercise, in which passengers earn Cruisercise dollars by participating in activities. There are several kinds of activities, and the Cruisercise cash can later be used to buy Cruisercise-logo wear in the gift shop. In addition, it's a lot of fun. Activities start at 7:00 or 7:30 in the morning with the Walk-a-Mile. On every cruise, you'll usually see at least one group of people walking on the top deck for forty minutes or so. It's a good way to strike up acquaintances. The ships also offer Stretch-Tone classes and aerobic classes.

The great thing about a cruise is that there is so much you can do if you want to. When at sea, make sure you know what activities are going on that day. Check your shipboard newspaper, the *Princess Patter*, which is delivered every night to your door. The staff will have activities going on all the time, and singles should definitely go to some of them. Don't stay in your room. The more you get out and participate, the more fun you will have.

BEST BETS FOR MEETING PEOPLE

When you cruise, you are automatically in an environment where it is very easy to meet people. You will more than likely become friends with your tablemates and do things with them while in port. "I think you get a real sense of companionship through your dinner mates," says Biggins. Princess advises that the young single sign up for the second seating at dinner (the first seating tends to be for older passengers).

If you choose to eat meals from the buffet, you multiply your chances of meeting new people. Just choose your table, and you will be joined by others. It's more casual, it's quicker, and it's not as much of an event as going to the dining room.

The pizzerias are nice, because you can go in and grab a pizza and sit with new people. Many single cruisers have met a lot of people this way. It's a great place to strike up conversations. The pizzerias are open during the day and into the late hours.

If you go to the dining room for lunch, you can also choose to sit with new people, since lunch seating is open. Don't be shy. People are always sharing tables. That is part of what cruising is all about.

Every cruise offers many activities that singles can participate in. This is a key way to get to know people and to develop relationships. On the first night, Princess holds a captain's party to welcome you aboard, and you can definitely find new friends there. Be sure to attend the singles get-together, which is usually held the first or second night. There may be two singles parties on longer cruises.

Dancing is one activity that attracts younger singles. Another area where people get to know others is the casino. The ships have lots of other evening activities that involve passenger participation, like a Name That Tune game and trivia quizzes.

During the day, singles can meet people in "mingle mode" by the bar. Stay in the central area of the main pools, which is probably where most conversation and activity will be taking place. People *want* to meet people on a cruise, and sometimes they develop long-lasting relationships.

Singles can also meet people in the hot tub or in the gym. Those who go to the gym tend to do so every day or every other day, so you can see the same faces. Also, you may want to participate in some of the exercise classes.

"I just got a letter from a woman in Canada," says Biggins. "She met a man on board one of our ships, and they are getting married." Guess where they are going for their honeymoon—on a cruise, of course! There are many Love Boat–type stories, but remember, there is no guarantee that you will find love on board a cruise ship.

On the smaller ships, you will get to know people because you will see them more. It also seems a bit easier to strike up a conversation on the smaller ships because of that intimate feeling.

On a big ship, unfortunately, you can run into someone the first day and not see that person again until days later. So if you are traveling on a large ship, find out names and cabin numbers when you have the chance. Give these people a call. The Caribbean cruises are on the larger ships, and because they have a lot more to offer, they will probably have more singles on board. The smaller ships usually offer the exotic cruises to such places as Asia, the South Pacific, India, and Africa.

Single men and women should introduce themselves to the cruise director. Say something like, "I am traveling by myself, and I am really interested in meeting people. Do you have any suggestions for me?" The cruise director and the maitre d' are really good people to get to know. They come in contact with many different people, and they will know who the other singles are. Be patient, however. It may take them a day or two to help you out.

ᐯERSONAL SAFETY

Cruising on a Princess ship is such a friendly experience that single passengers don't really feel they are out on their own and instead feel well taken care of. If there is a problem, a crew member will always be there to help you.

If you want to go on a shore excursion, women in particular should know that all Princess tours are run by the company. All are all checked out thoroughly for safety and security. Princess maintains very close relations with all its tour operations, so it has a very strong, highly regarded tour program. "I think they all have something nice to offer," says Biggins.

Wherever and whenever possible, air-conditioned traveling coaches are used for Princess tours. It's a safe way to go, and it's comfortable. Even if you are traveling by yourself, while on a tour you will be on a bus or in some kind of safe transportation. You'll be with other passengers, and it's a nice way to see the islands, ports, and cities that Princess visits. The cruise line does *not* recommend going off by yourself on shore. Go with at least one other person.

One of the benefits of going on a tour is that Princess will always know where you are. For example, if a bus is running late and the ship is supposed to sail at 5:00, you don't have to worry.

The ship won't leave until all the buses from all the tours get back. If you go off independently, on the other hand, and you are not back, the cruise line has no way of knowing that you aren't there. If you do take that chance, be responsible and get back in plenty of time.

Single women should remember that on a cruise, they are safe. Travel on land, which usually involves hotels, rental cars, and taxis, doesn't always offer women a sense of safety. Cruising does. On a cruise, the restaurants and entertainment are all included, along with a built-in sense of security. Everything is arranged for you. "I could not recommend a better type of vacation for a single woman—or for a single man, of course," says Biggins.

THEME AND SPECIAL-INTEREST CRUISES

Cruising can be a mystery to people who have never done it before, since they don't really know what to expect. So you may want to consider taking a shorter cruise before you take a seven-day cruise to see if you will like it. Princess has an affordable way for singles to do this, called Love Boat Samplers. These shorter two-, three-, and four-day cruises are offered every fall and spring, when Princess repositions its ships up the West Coast for the Alaska season. This can provide a very enjoyable first-cruise experience.

PRECRUISE INFORMATION

Your travel agent is a real ally in making your cruise plans. The agent is the communication link between the passenger and the cruise line. Princess enters into a computer all the information that the agent has gathered, and from that a report goes to the ship. The maitre d', for instance, looks up all the special request forms. If Princess knows that a single person is looking forward to meeting other people, then the dining room staff will try to seat that person accordingly.

If you want the second seating for dinner, which is the more popular seating on any cruise, you should put in for that early. Otherwise, you will be on a wait list. It's really difficult to get late seating on the Caribbean cruises in particular if you don't book early.

Singles should take advantage of Love Boat Savers and the early booking incentives this program offers. They get a better value for their cruise dollar at the time they book (rates go up rather than down as a sailing date approaches). If a promotion rate becomes available on that sailing, the single man or woman who has booked early may qualify for that lower rate. For the Europe and Alaska cruises, Princess offers an early booking deadline that gives the best savings. For the Caribbean cruises, Princess has a rate of 50 percent off for the second person.

If you want to get your choice sailing date, you certainly want to book early.

NEW AND FUTURE POSSIBILITIES

When the *Grand Princess* makes her debut in May 1998, a virtual paradise-at-sea will be available for singles. You will be able to dine in any of her eight dining areas, gamble in the largest casino afloat, and dance in the disco suspended fifteen decks above the water. And while balcony cabins are still a limited feature on most non-Princess cruise ships, 80 percent of the 928 cabins do include balconies, more than any other ship afloat.

Princess has announced a financing program that addresses the number one consumer issue in the cruise industry today: the perception that a cruise is unaffordable. The Princess Love Boat Loan program now makes cruising affordable to everyone and brings these dream vacations within reach. Love Boat Loan has been developed to offer travelers immediate and convenient contact with banks providing the special lines of credit for a virtually instant credit decision.

Interested individuals can access the financing program by calling (800) PRINCESS, or, if they are in their travel agent's office, they can be transferred to the bank from the Princess reservation department. Consumers can finance everything from deposit through final payment (other than a $50 per person nonrefundable down payment). They can choose a repayment schedule of twenty-four, thirty-six, or forty-eight months, as suits their budget. The Love Boat Loan line of credit can be used not only for cruises but also for cruise tours, Cruise Plus packages, airfare provided through Princess, and even onboard spending.

Since Love Boat Loan is actually a line of credit, consumers will not have to pay off the full balance from their cruise purchase in order to cruise again. As long as there is still credit available and the consumer still meets the bank's requirements, the line of credit may be used to finance another cruise. "Our passengers can take another cruise sooner than they otherwise would or perhaps take a long cruise to a more exotic destination," says Biggins.

CHAPTER 11

ℛoyal Caribbean Cruise Lines

1050 Caribbean Way
Miami, FL 33132
Telephone (305) 539-6000 or (800) 255-4373
On-line address: www.royalcaribbean.com

"Royal Caribbean is one of the world's largest cruise lines" says Rich Steck, manager of public relations for Royal Caribbean Cruise Lines. He believes that cruising in general is a great way to meet people, because there are lots of people to choose from. If you find that you don't really care for one person, there is always someone else. It's safe on a cruise. You don't have to pack and unpack and drag your luggage around or drive all over town. "A ship is a city in miniature, so you've got lots of opportunity to meet others."

𝒢ENERAL SHIP INFORMATION

Royal Caribbean owns eleven modern ships with a total capacity of 19,770 berths. Through 1998, the company will introduce the last three of its six Vision class ships, adding a capacity of 5,950 passengers. The fleet includes *Sovereign of the Seas*, the *Nordic Empress*, the *Viking Serenade*, the *New Grandeur of the Seas*, the *Monarch of the Seas*, the *Majesty of the Seas*, and the *Rhapsody of the Seas*, which is a brand new ship holding 2,000 passengers. The *Legend of the Seas* holds 1,804 (not to mention an eighteen-hole golf course).

DESTINATIONS, LENGTH OF CRUISES, DEPARTURE PORTS

The award-winning Royal Caribbean fleet offers passengers sixty-six different itineraries and 156 destinations and attractions, including Alaska, the Bahamas, Bermuda, the Caribbean, Europe, Southeast Asia and the Far East, Hawaii, Mexico, Panama Canal, Russia, and Scandinavia.

Royal Caribbean offers a short cruise aboard the *Sovereign of the Seas*. It leaves every Friday from Miami for the Bahamas, and it returns on Monday. It then departs again for a four-night cruise back to the Bahamas, and it comes back on Friday. This cruise is very popular with young singles.

The *New Grandeur of the Seas* sails to the eastern Caribbean from Miami every Saturday. The *Monarch of the Seas* cruises from San Juan, Puerto Rico, to the southern Caribbean every Sunday. Or you can sail on the *Majesty of the Seas* every Sunday to the western Caribbean from Miami. Of these, the *Monarch* will be a little more expensive, because you have to pay the additional air-fare to get to San Juan, which is quite a distance away.

The line's *Nordic Empress* sails three- and four-night southern Caribbean cruises from San Juan in the winter and from Port Canaveral to the Bahamas in the summer. The *Viking Serenade* sails out of Los Angeles to Ensenada and San Diego and back over four nights. Those are probably the two most popular cruises for young singles.

Other popular cruises for singles are the seven-night Caribbean cruises, which feature beaches, sunshine, and days at sea. Royal Caribbean has seven-night cruises aboard the *Legend of the Seas* and the *Rhapsody of the Seas*. In the summer, it has seven-night cruises out of New York that go to Bermuda.

Where do *you* want to go? Steck insists that is a very individual question. "It depends on your lifestyle—and that is where a travel agent, somebody who knows Royal Caribbean's itineraries and ports of call, can really be helpful." For younger people, Steck believes that almost any Caribbean itinerary would do well, because there are lots of water sports, beach activities, and good shopping.

For people who want a more cultural vacation, Steck recommends Alaska, Europe, or Asia. For people who want a mix of culture, adventure, and shopping, Steck suggests Bermuda.

Royal Caribbean has a special share program for single travelers. The cruise line will arrange for you to share a cabin (at the lowest rate) with another person of the same sex and smoking preference. If a roommate is not found for you, you will travel solo in the cabin and even be upgraded to a nicer cabin if available.

PASSENGER INFORMATION

Younger singles are going to be attracted to the shorter cruises, especially if they are first-time cruisers. Also, the weekend cruises tend to be spur-of-the-moment events. "When I say young," says Steck, "I'm talking about singles in their twenties and thirties." The shorter cruises are relatively inexpensive, which fits the pocketbooks of singles in that age bracket. Those that do have more money will take the seven-day cruises.

Alaska is more popular for older singles in their forties and up. Europe also attracts the older single traveler, because it is more expensive and the cruises are twelve and fourteen nights in length. It really takes two weeks for those destinations. Royal Caribbean also has a ship in Asia offering fourteen-night cruises, which would also probably attract the older single. Bermuda is not generally viewed as an exciting, adventurous place, but it's wonderful nonetheless, and a lot of more sophisticated single travelers opt for it.

Singles have to be honest about their expectations about cruising. Are they going because they want to get away and just decompress for a while, or are they looking for some romance and adventure? "It's important to know what your expectations are when thinking about a cruise," says Steck. You'll meet the right kind of person if you go on the right kind of cruise. For example, if you are interested in meeting somebody you can talk to, you should consider a cruise to Alaska, where you might meet singles who are interested in other things besides looking great on the beach.

A question that arises when singles travel is whether to travel alone or with a friend. Steck does not feel that it makes much difference. It depends on why you want to travel. If you are looking for romance, then you should probably go alone—you just may find what you are looking for. If, however, you are going for an enjoyable vacation, it might be nice to have a single friend along, because you are then assured of companionship. You have a built-in companion to do things with, and it takes the pressure off the need to look for partners. You have to really know why you are taking the cruise.

Older single women are more apt to travel as a pair, because there is the comfort of security. Even when traveling alone, women can find other solo women travelers and make arrangements to meet in the disco, go together on a shore excursion, or go to the beach together. In the company of a friend, whether you meet on the cruise or have been friends forever, cruising can be really nice.

"Cruising is like real life," says Steck. "A ship is really a macrocosm of a small city. We can't say that you are going to find the man or woman of your dreams on a cruise, or you're going to find love and romance—because you may not. But you will have a good time as long as you don't become desperate about being alone. In that case, you are *not* going to have a good time. You won't have a good time back home either, so it is really your psychological state that counts."

ONBOARD LIFE

After you have found your cabin and unpacked, you might want to look over the ship. Steck suggests going to the ship's library and checking things out there. You should also go to the shops, which will open as soon as the ship leaves the pier. People are always going in and out of the shops. Also, be sure to peek in at the lounges.

The dining room is a great place to meet others. Your travel agent can help you get a good table. Remember, a travel agent is *your* agent, not the cruise line's agent. Tell your agent that you want to be at a dining table with singles your age. The agent will then relay that information to the cruise line. After you board, you can still make dining room reservations if you have not arranged them through your travel agent.

Royal Caribbean tries to get as much information as it can about passengers so that the computer—which really does the dining room seating arrangements—can then place people at an appropriate table. However, the dining room manager always holds back some seats and tables, because invariably a few people are not happy with the computer's arrangements. "Never hesitate to go to the dining room manager if you do not like your table and want to move," says Steck.

A good way to have fun and perhaps meet new people is to talk to the cruise staff. Staff members are told to keep an eye out, especially for the single people. Just remember that for the most part, the goal of every shipboard employee is to make sure you have a good time. If you wish, they will try to introduce you to other single people—not with an eye for matchmaking, but simply in order to maximize your cruise experience. You will have a better time if you meet somebody with whom you can share your good times. No one wants you to leave the ship disappointed.

The cruise staff usually wears identifying uniforms so you can tell who they are. They are usually young, and they are usually American or English. Just tell them that you are traveling as a single and that you would appreciate an introduction to anyone else they might come across who is also traveling single. It's as simple as that. Even though Royal Caribbean's ships can be huge, the staff members keep their eyes open. They are professionals who do this week after week after week. Within hours of embarking on each new cruise, they know who is single and who is not.

The cruise director and the hostess are two especially good people to approach. They are the number one and two most helpful people on the cruise staff. The sports director and the shore excursion people are also there to help you.

The maitre d' and the head waiter routinely survey the dining room the first night out and determine, among other things, where the young singles and the middle-aged singles are sitting.

Part of their job is to find out who is sitting where and what kind of people they have on the cruise. There are always types within cruises: party types, serious types, and so forth. Royal Caribbean's staff realizes this, and the chances are very good that some changes can be made to get you where you need to be to enjoy your cruising experience to the utmost. If your travel agent has not been able to organize certain details for you initially, then the cruise ship staff will.

There are days when the dining room will feature open seating for breakfast and lunch, which means you can take a seat anywhere. You should take advantage of this chance to move around and scout out people you have not had the chance to meet yet. Open seating usually is allowed when the ship is in port. When you go to the dining room for an open-seating meal, you should let your waiter know that you would like to sit with single people your age. If the waiter knows of an appropriate table, you will be seated there, if possible.

There are two formal nights on the one-week cruises. Formal means "nice." For men, tuxedos are optional, but you will see about 30 percent of the men in them. Women may wish to wear a nice cocktail gown—not a ball gown, just a nice, dressy outfit. "A formal gown is not necessary," says Steck.

The ships have some casual-dress evenings for which a skirt and blouse would be appropriate for women, and sport shirts and slacks for men. Swimwear with a wraparound or cover-up, however, is not appropriate. And remember, Royal Caribbean does have dry cleaning and laundry services aboard for reasonable fees.

You will definitely need sports clothes for daytime wear. Shorts on the islands are okay in the Caribbean but not necessarily elsewhere. For women, slacks or a skirt are always a good idea. You are always safe with pants. Don't forget to pack a pair of sensible walking shoes, particularly if you plan to take any walking excursions.

All kinds of activities are offered on every Royal Caribbean cruise ship. You can attend lectures, bingo games, or dance classes. First, you should check your activity program the night before and make a list of what you would like to do the next day. For example, you may decide to visit the gym before breakfast, join an exercise class, and then relax in the spa. The gym is a good place to meet people, and it is easy to strike up a conversation with the person exercising next to you.

For the rest of your day at sea, you might decide to have a late breakfast, either a buffet or seated in the dining room. Then you can go to the pool deck and swim a little and stroll a little. Take a look at the jogging track. Wandering back to the pool area, you can order something refreshing at the bar. This is another place that is conducive to meeting people and chatting. It is a comfortable and natural atmosphere where you can share stories and information. Then it's time for the luncheon buffet or lunch in the dining room.

There are all sorts of activities in the afternoon. One day there might be a wine tasting. That always means a good time for a wide range of ages and levels of sophistication. Younger singles, in their twenties and thirties, go to become more sophisticated at judging wines. Older singles, in their forties and up, go to learn more about the offered vintages. It's a wonderful opportunity for casual conversations. "Just keep your eyes open and see who's with and who's without," suggests Steck.

Certain ages gravitate towards certain lounges on board. For example, the disco is where younger singles congregate, especially after dinner and after the evening show. Royal Caribbean has a schooner bar on its ships, which is a piano bar, and it is popular with young people as well as middle-aged people. Older singles are more likely to go to lounges in the late afternoon or early evening for a predinner cocktail.

One nice thing to do on a cruise vacation is to get dressed (according to the code for the evening) early and visit one of the ship's bars before dinner. The Viking Crown Lounge is one place you shouldn't miss. After dinner, it becomes a disco and gets pretty loud and noisy, but before dinner it is a nice little place to have a quiet cocktail. You'll find a Viking Crown Lounge on every ship. The line's bigger ships have a rather elegant place called the Champagne Bar, where you can enjoy champagne, better wines, and caviar. You will see a lot of people there, and it gets the evening off to a very special start. After dinner, you can go to the show, to one of the lounges, or to the casino. Many single people enjoy gaming in the casino.

Singles should always check out the daily program, which will be slipped under their door every night by their cabin steward. It will list all the activities for the next day. Check it out, decide where you want to go and what you want to do, and then plan your day accordingly.

BEST BETS FOR MEETING PEOPLE

Singles who are serious about meeting new people should try to go to every activity, at least initially. Most ships have a singles get-together early in the cruise. That is a must. Sometimes these events are held the first night. It is an icebreaker, and you will get to meet a lot of single people there.

Also, go to the pool area and just hang out. You will find a lot of singles near the pool bars, especially near the calypso bands that play on the pool deck during the day. Many singles looking for new friends sit near the bars, having sodas or the fancy umbrella drinks of the day. That is a key place for singles to congregate.

Steck encourages single cruisers not to eat breakfast in their rooms. If they are looking for a less formal meal than what the dining room offers, they can always have breakfast or lunch on deck, where there is a buffet. They then can look around, see who else is sitting alone, and take that opportunity to make a new acquaintance. In fact, if you aren't watching your waistline too seriously, you could conceivably enjoy a very light buffet on deck, then order a regular meal in the dining room. Anything is possible when cruising! This way, you can observe your fellow passengers. At night, you can go up to the midnight buffet. "Don't have your dinner sent to your cabin," says Steck.

The shipboard dance classes seem to attract many singles, and you can see right away who has a partner and who doesn't. Ask the shore excursion manager what kinds of activities attract single people on your particular cruise. The shore excursion staff will be glad to make suggestions on which shore tour or activity would be your best bet. They can help you.

Steck gives one last and very unusual tip: "At the lifeboat drill, they generally call out cabin numbers, and the occupants call out how many are in that cabin. If a voice calls out 'One,' try to spot that person."

SHORE EXCURSIONS

Some singles love beach fun. A beach can be found at every port of call in the Caribbean, and Royal Caribbean has three megaships covering the Caribbean year-round.

Whatever your idea of fun, plan your shore excursions well in advance. The shore excursion desk opens the first day—actually the first night, generally after the lifeboat drill.

If your shore excursions are going to include shopping, Steck recommends that you have in mind before the cruise what you want to buy. Before leaving home, go to the best discount store offering that particular item and see what it costs. Then see what that item costs on board in the ship's stores. Then go downtown in one of the shopping ports and see what the item costs there. Buy wherever the best price is offered. Steck feels that often you'll find the ship's stores will give you the best deal. "The shops on board our ships are not a concession, and they can sell merchandise at bargain prices."

Be careful of island prices that are too good to be true; you could be disappointed later. Royal Caribbean, like most other cruise lines, has a program in which it encourages passengers to patronize onshore stores that will meet the line's qualifications. The stores do pay a fee for this service, which is comparable to broadcast or newspaper advertising. The stores must meet certain criteria, and Royal Caribbean is honest about telling people that the shops it recommends are part of a promotional program. It works to everyone's benefit, including the passengers. If you shop at one of the recommended shops and later find that the diamond you bought is not what you were led to believe, Royal Caribbean will insist that the shop make amends or refund your money. The cruise line will not hesitate to use its power on your behalf. If you buy at an store that is not recommended, however, and back home you discover the diamond is not what you were told, then Royal Caribbean cannot help you. The program ensures that you have the protection of the cruise line's endorsement.

PERSONAL SAFETY

Singles traveling alone, especially single women, have to face the question of safety. If you sample six different bars in a strange city, it can definitely be dangerous, but you are always safe on a cruise ship. "Cruising offers a wonderful opportunity for singles," says Steck.

When you go ashore to shop or tour, Steck suggests that at all times you travel with somebody else. "Another person or a small group is always better than venturing off alone. You never know who is looking for an easy target, someone who will be here today and gone tomorrow, so travel in a crowd. On tours and on ship-sponsored shore excursions, you are always in a safe group. That is much better than going off on your own."

CRUISING SEASONS

When is the best time for singles to take a Royal Caribbean cruise? Summers are always good, because that's vacation time, the universal season for younger singles. In the wintertime, passengers tend to be a bit older. "I think that in the winter a lot of singles want to go skiing, so summers are better for the younger set," says Steck. He advises that you go by the itinerary, remembering this formula: shorter cruises, younger cruisers; longer cruises, older cruisers.

NEW AND FUTURE POSSIBILITIES

In 1999, Royal Caribbean will introduce the first of its 3,100-passenger Eagle class ships. A second Eagle ship will follow in the year 2000.

CHAPTER 12

ℛoyal Olympic Cruises

(represented by Sun Line Cruises)
I Rockefeller Plaza
New York, NY 10020
Telephone (800) 872-6400

Royal Olympic Cruises is the largest cruise line the Mediterranean. Formed in 1995 by the merger of Sun Line Cruises and Epirotiki Cruise Line, the company boasts nearly a century of combined maritime experience. "This is a record no other cruise line in the region can match," says Meg Duncan, director of public relations.

ℊENERAL SHIP INFORMATION

Royal Olympic has six ships, which are distinguished by their attention to a personal atmosphere and culinary-enriching itineraries. From April through November all three ships operate in the Mediterranean; from December through March, the line offers cruises to South America.

The line's ships are smaller than average, so you get a sense of community within just a few days. Also, the ships feature a high crew-to-passenger service ratio—almost two passengers for every crew member. The staff gets to know you quickly, adding a special sense of hospitality and friendliness.

DESTINATIONS, LENGTH OF CRUISES, DEPARTURE PORTS

In the summer, the focus of Royal Olympic's programs is the Aegean and eastern Mediterranean, where Royal Olympic is the dominant cruise line in the area. Cruises range from three to twenty-one days, and feature calls in the Greek islands, combined with either Turkey, Egypt, Israel, or ports in the Black Sea. Several new itineraries are being introduced, among them a series of fourteen-day Western Europe cruises between Copenhagen and Athens, plus fourteen-day Baltic, North Cape, and Scandinavia cruises that sail round-trip from Copenhagen.

Royal Olympic has so many different destinations that where you choose to go depends on your personal interests. Duncan believes, judging by the volume of business enjoyed by Royal Olympic's forebears, that the Mediterranean is one of the "hottest" cruise destinations. It is a matter of personal preference which ports you might like, because there is so much to see and do in the Mediterranean. There truly is something for everybody in every port.

In the winter, two ships reposition to the Americas. The *Stella Solaris* features holiday cruises from Fort Lauderdale, as well as cruises to Brazil, which showcase the Amazon river. The ship then repositions to Galveston, Texas. "From Galveston, we offer a number of cruises to the Caribbean, Panama Canal, and land of the Maya" says Duncan. "On the *Odysseus,* we feature two-week cruises to the Straits of Magellan and Cape Horn/Falkland Islands, both of which highlight the tip of South America. Then in the spring, we reposition ourselves back to Greece to start our Mediterranean cruises again."

ᴾASSENGER INFORMATION

Royal Olympic doesn't attract many young singles. The destinations of the cruises—the Mediterranean and South America—are considered a bit "high ticket" and are more culturally oriented. Even if you go on a three-day cruise, starting at $500, it will probably cost you an additional $1,200 to $1,500 for the airfare and land package. Generally, people spend between $1,800 and $2,500 per person on the Mediterranean cruises or tour packages, which is high for the three-day-cruise-out-of-Miami crowd. Royal Olympic cruises appeal more to the older singles group. "I would say we don't get many in the twenty-to-thirty group," says Duncan. "Our passengers are more like thirty-five and up."

ᴼNBOARD LIFE

A typical winter-month cruise day begins with breakfast in the dining room. You might want to bring the daily program with you. This will have been slipped under your door the night before. It tells you all the different activities for the day and gives you something to read if you happen to be the first person to arrive at your table. It will also serve as an opener to discuss the activities with people you meet at breakfast. It will help you plot your day, and perhaps you will find someone who would like to join you in one or more of the activities in which you are interested.

You might want to take a dance class, attend a lecture, or go to a movie. Plot out your day. After an activity in the morning, you may want to get in a little pure rest and relaxation before lunch. After all, you are on vacation. So you might pick a deck chair in a nice spot and read a book until lunchtime. Have lunch in the dining room or on deck, as you please. Look at your activity program for the afternoon. What might be of interest to you? There are usually two or three activities going on at the same time, so there is never a lack of something to do. Meanwhile, it is almost guaranteed that you will meet people with whom you can strike up a conversation.

Your travel agent should have informed the maitre d' of your status and dinner table preference before you boarded, but if not, let the maitre d' know your preference immediately. The larger the table, the larger circle of people you can get to know. "Let's face it," says Duncan, "not everyone on a cruise is going to be your best friend. But if you have six or seven people at your table, the chances of finding someone you will get along with are greater than if you sit at a table for four."

Dinner dress will vary throughout the cruise. There are formal nights, informal nights, and casual nights. Before you board your ship, you will receive a schedule telling you how many formal nights there will be and which nights they are, along with dress code guidelines.

Dress codes seem to be more flexible these days. Formal night is no longer strictly tuxedos and ball gowns. It can be a dark suit for the gentleman and a cocktail dress for the lady. Informal nights is a suit or jacket and tie for the man and a dress or skirt for the woman. Casual nights is a jacket or just a sport shirt with slacks for the man and a skirt or slacks and a blouse for the woman.

The beginning of any cruise will probably have a welcome aboard party with icebreaker activities. This is a good opportunity for the single cruiser to make new acquaintances, especially for the sort of person who participates in fun (okay, silly, sometimes downright goofy) games. You may be chosen to get up and do a dance with a balloon. You may or may not win a prize, but you certainly get to meet people.

If your ship is going to be in port at seven o'clock in the morning, then breakfast might not be served on deck, but it is served in the dining room every day. You can receive breakfast in your cabin every day except the last day of the cruise. For lunch, there is always a buffet on deck plus service in the dining room.

If you just want to get away from everybody, order breakfast in your room. If you want to meet as many people as possible, you should eat breakfast and lunch in the dining room. Those are open-seating meals, and the maitre d' will escort you to a seat where you will meet new people.

At night, passengers go to the lounge to see the show. You will find a good number of people there. The passenger traveling alone can naturally ask if a seat is taken and can readily be invited to sit with a group.

On the *Stella Solaris*, Royal Olympic provides dance hosts for single women needing partners. They tend to be older gentlemen. Their job on board—if you want to call it a job—is to mix and mingle, but primarily to dance. The cruise features a lot of dancing on board, including the shows in the lounges. "They will know who the single women are," says Duncan, or women whose husbands don't like to dance, and offer them a chance to get out on the dance floor. The dance hosts also fill in at social events. For instance, they will be at the singles cocktail parties, and they will be on certain tours. They might fill in at a bridge game. They are passengers, but they are also there to help out in certain social situations. Men in these positions come on board for limited periods. One might sign on for a month, then go home. Most of them are retired and/or widowed. Royal Olympic gets a lot of comments from people regarding its dance host program; many have written the entertainment director to say that they had not danced since their husbands died, and it was wonderful to be asked to dance again.

Then there is the regular cruise staff. Staff members will be at the singles cocktail hour as part of their job. Several social hostesses will also be on board. If someone is not having a good time (which is very rare), these hostesses will try to figure out how to solve the problem. Any passenger can approach a social hostess with a social problem. For instance, if you want to play bridge but don't have a partner, let the hostess know. The hostess may have been approached by someone else looking for a partner. She can put the two of you together, or she might find one of the dance hosts who can also play bridge.

ℬEST BETS FOR MEETING PEOPLE

If your object is to meet people, the smaller size of Royal Olympic's ships should be appealing. You are not going to get lost here, as you might in a megaship.

It is a completely subjective decision to travel by yourself or with another person. It depends somewhat on the type of travel you are doing. However, Duncan assures us, "I think you're perfectly fine traveling by yourself, because there's a natural tendency for socializing on a cruise." Everyone is—literally—in the same boat, and it is very easy to meet people to strike up conversations. You don't have to rely on bringing your own companion. For example, you'll be seated with other people at dinner, so you don't have to worry about eating alone. On Royal Olympic cruises there is always a cocktail party for singles at the beginning of the cruise so that singles can meet each other. You will also meet people on the different tours you take. You will run into people on deck, in the dining room, in the lounges, and at the shows. Joining one of the fitness classes is one way to meet people. It is very easy to make pleasant acquaintances, if not best friends.

Be bold. If you choose to eat on deck, you may wind up eating alone unless you ask to share a table with someone. If you go into the dining room, the maitre d' will escort you to a table where people are already sitting. You will probably all arrive at about the same time, so you will all be ordering together. This can be another way to meet a lot of people. You can meet different people every day. As mentioned earlier, bring your daily activity guide along to breakfast to serve as an opener for inviting someone to join you in one or more of the activities.

One way to meet people during cruises is to take a tour in port. Go on a shore excursion. You will be in a group of about thirty people. Just the sort of person you want to meet may sit next to you on the bus. While you are touring, you might strike up a conversation with any of your fellow travelers. "You will probably meet a lot of people on the tours," says Duncan.

SHORE EXCURSIONS

"There is something for everyone in the Mediterranean," says Duncan. You can learn about fantastic cultural and social histories—the cradle of democracy and the very birth of western civilization is here. On top of that, it's beautiful, warm, and sunny, so you can visit beaches on the Greek islands without worrying about the weather. If you want to shop, you can go to Istanbul,

Rhodes, Damascus—all have beautiful shops. If you want to visit historic sites, you will certainly find plenty of those.

Generally, you should take the prepared tours, particularly in Royal Olympic's destinations in the Mediterranean, where there is so much history. "If you are interested in history, you are better off on a tour escorted by a guide who can give you as much information as you need," says Duncan. "I find that when I go on my own, I often miss a lot, because I'm not knowledgeable enough to know what to look for." When you take a tour escorted by a licensed guide who is trained and knowledgeable, you will get a lot more out of your visit. If the main reason you are visiting the destination is to learn about the ancient Greek ruins (or to visit the palace of the Crusaders, or Bethlehem, or Cairo), you should consider taking a tour.

CRUISING SEASONS

Actually, there is no particular season—summer, Christmas, or whatever—when any one of Royal Olympic's cruises is more popular among singles. Passengers are likely to spend more time on board during the winter months, because there are more days at sea on such cruises as the Amazon, transatlantic (from the Mediterranean to Fort Lauderdale), and Panama Canal cruises.

TIPPING

Tipping is very easy on a Royal Olympic ship. "People love our tipping system," Duncan says, "because you don't have to walk around at the end of the cruise with a dozen different envelopes."

Because these are Greek ships, the crews work under Greek steward union rules, which say that all tips are pooled for the crew. So everyone, even people who work behind the scenes, receives a portion of the tips. The busboys, the people in the back, the bartenders, the wine stewards—everyone is part of the pool.

Royal Olympic recommends an amount of $9 per passenger per day. At the end of the cruise, you deposit your tip at the chief steward's desk, who will take care of distributing all the gratuities based on the regulations of the union.

$\mathcal{W}$indjammer Barefoot Cruises

PO Box 190120
Miami, FL 33119
Telephone (305) 534-7447 or (800) 327-2601

"We are kind of a bed-and-breakfast at sea," says Michael Vegis, director of public relations for Windjammer Barefoot Cruises. "We have been sailing since 1947, and now we have the largest fleet of privately owned small ships."

Windjammer Barefoot Cruises is run by the Burke family. Mike Burke, founder of the line, has turned over the day-to-day helm of the company to his son and daughter. His son runs operations, and his daughter handles the marketing, advertising, and reservations, so it is very much a family concern. A lot of things are done simply because that's the way they have always been done. On the other hand, this line does a lot of wonderful and innovative things because no one knew they weren't supposed to do them.

Perhaps even more interesting is the fact that Windjammer books several singles-only cruises each year. Most singles find out about them from brochures and press releases and a great deal of word of mouth. "Most of our bookings, believe it or not, are

119

word of mouth," Vegis says. The company did a study and discovered that it has a 40 percent repeat-passenger rate. "That figure might even be a bit low," claims Vegis, "because I have never been on a ship where less than half of the people had not been on one of our cruises before."

GENERAL SHIP INFORMATION

Windjammer sails classic tall ships, whose previous owners have been folks like the Vanderbilts, E. F. Hutton, the Duke of Westminster, and Aristotle Onassis. Each ship has an interesting past. Take, for instance, the *Fantome*. Aristotle Onassis bought it as a wedding present for Princess Grace and Prince Rainier of Monaco. However, the prince and the princess did not invite him to the wedding, so he never gave them the ship. That's how Windjammer got it.

The *Fantome* is the line's biggest ship at 282 feet long. Windjammer just finished a $6 million refurbishment of all the cabin and passenger areas on the *Fantome*. Now the cabins are a bit bigger, with bigger beds, making them more appealing to couples, particularly honeymooners. The *Polynesia* is 248 feet and holds 126 passengers. You might have seen the *Mandalay*, which holds seventy-two passengers, in an American Express commercial. In the commercial, a husband and wife are boating and the wife is having a miserable time. A sail falls on her head. Just then, she sees the *Mandalay* coming around the point. "We also had the BBC on board the *Mandalay* recently," says Vegis. "They filmed for two days, producing a segment for their program called *Holidays*."

Windjammer ships are more intimate than are the ships of most cruise lines. Its entire fleet would fit on one level of a megaship. Except for the *Amazing Grace*, which is the line's supply ship, all Windjammer ships have sails. The *Amazing Grace* also carries passengers as she supplies the tall ships.

Other ships include the *Flying Cloud*, which holds seventy-four passengers. She was a navy cadet training ship for the French before Windjammer got her. The *Yankee Clipper* holds sixty-four passengers.

DESTINATIONS, LENGTH OF CRUISES, DEPARTURE PORTS

Windjammer tries to place its ships in areas to suit each ship's advantages. Windjammer's best sailing ship, the small *Yankee Clipper*, is in the Grenadines, a relatively isolated beach destination. The *Clipper* will sail into places such as the resort island of Palm Island and Tobago Cays, a group of deserted—or at least uninhabited—islands with some of the best diving and snorkeling in the Caribbean.

"There are very few cruises down in the Grenadines," Vegis says. It is undiscovered. Ports of call include the old whaling port of Bequia, which is Vegis's favorite island. There is a walkway right around the bay, where all the restaurants and shops are located. You can also do some snorkeling there. The cruise line also goes to Young Island, just off of St. Vincent.

The *Yankee Clipper* sails from Grenada to Carriacou, Palm Island, Bequia, and Canouan. Carriacou is fairly big, with a population of three or four hundred people. It is actually one of the three islands that make up the country of Grenada. Palm Island is probably no more than a mile in circumference. It is just a little island that happens to have a very upscale resort. The owner is a good friend of Captain Burke, the owner of Windjammer Cruises, so the ships often spend the day there. Canouan is a fairly new addition that Captain Burke has decided to visit with his cruises. From there, the *Clipper* visits some of the better-known islands. It spends a day in St. Lucia, a day in Martinique, a day in Dominica, and Isles De Saints, which is a little group of islands south of Guadeloupe. Then it sails into Antigua.

The *Mandalay* leaves from Grenada the first Monday of the month for a two-week cruise up to Antigua. On the third Monday of the month, she leaves from Antigua for the two weeks back down to Grenada.

Since the *Flying Cloud* holds only seventy-four people, she is positioned in the British Virgin Islands, where she does not have to cover much territory. She does morning sails, usually of about three or four hours in duration.

The *Mandalay* offers a thirteen-day cruise between Antigua and Grenada. The *Amazing Grace*, the line's supply ship, also makes the thirteen-day trip between Antigua and Grenada. The *Polynesia* sails from St. Maarten to the islands of Anguilla, St. Bart's, and Nevis, which is a youth-oriented location. The *Fantome* sails from Belize City to Belize Reef, the Gulf of Honduras, and the Bay Island. This area is known as the Tahiti of the Northern Hemisphere.

ACCOMMODATIONS FOR SINGLES

Windjammer will match people to share a cabin. There is no single supplement. If you want to pay for a cabin by yourself for an in-season cruise, you will have to pay for two spaces. The rate for single occupancy during the off-season is 175 percent. However, during the off-season, there is a good possibility you might get a cabin by yourself anyway, because the ships usually sail at about

75 to 80 percent of capacity. If Windjammer cannot match you with a same-sex roommate, Vegis promises, "We will never force anyone to pay more than our regular cruise rate."

*P*ASSENGER INFORMATION

Sixty-five percent of Windjammer passengers are between thirty-five and fifty-five years old. The *Polynesia,* which tends to be more of a singles party ship, attracts people in their thirties to early forties. The line has all its singles cruises on this ship. It has a large capacity and a reputation for being a good party ship.

The *Yankee Clipper*'s cruises are just the thing for people who are really hard core about sailing and hanging out on beaches. The *Flying Cloud* tends to get people who are divers or snorkelers, because she sails into very good diving areas. The *Mandalay* and the *Amazing Grace* both make the trip between Antigua and Grenada, but the *Amazing Grace* tends to get a much older crowd aboard.

Other than age, the typical Windjammer cruiser has a certain style. Vegis sums up this style by comparing Windjammer ships to another line's ships: "They built their ships from the ground up and have cabins with TV sets and phones—stuff like that is anathema to our passengers." The idea of having a television set or even a phone on a Windjammer is totally against the nature of anyone who enjoys Windjammer.

*O*NBOARD LIFE

Let's get something straight here. One of the biggest misconceptions about this line is that people have to work on

Windjammer ships. This is not true. A day aboard one of the line's tall ships is not a day spent with a bucket, scrub brush, and bar of lye soap. If passengers want to help raise the big sails, they can certainly volunteer. They can take turns at the helm. That is the only work they will ever do.

Boarding is always on a Sunday night at five o'clock. The Windjammer crew brings aboard a steel or reggae band for a party with a buffet dinner, giving away rum swizzles, which is the house drink.

Windjammer's crews give informal sailing classes and knot-tying classes. One of the captains has a stand-up comedy routine, which he calls Magic Knot-Tying and Bondage Class. He does magic tricks with knots that he has learned over the years. That is the true atmosphere of a Windjammer cruise. "Our appeal is the Jimmy Buffet type, a laid-back Caribbean mentality," explains Vegis.

Everything is completely relaxed. It is, just as Vegis claims, like a bed-and-breakfast at sea. You get to know the captain, the mates, and all the rest of the crew, because you interact with them as much as you do with the other passengers.

Every night at sunset, you are offered swizzles, hors d'oeuvres, and other sunset cocktails. There is no formal night in the dining room. In fact, you never have to dress up at all. T-shirts, shorts, and swimsuits are the order of the day. They do have a captain's dinner, for which they suggest that everyone wear a *clean* T-shirt. That is about as dressed up as you get. The captain himself is likely to go barefoot about the deck. You can't get any more unstuffy than that.

There is no assigned seating for any meal. For dinner, seating is strictly first come, first served. No pressure. Lunches are served buffet-style on the top deck, though often they have beach picnics. Breakfast is served as you wander in from your cabin. Staff will serve you any time before noon. There is no set hour.

There are no hard-and-fast rules to follow aboard a Wind-jammer. Once you are on board, the only thing that you ever have to do is participate in a safety drill on the first day. After that, you are on your own. You can do as much or as little as you want. There will be parties and fun activities like crab races. Crab races? "We draw a circle on deck," Vegis explains, "then we have crabs that we number, and we take bets on them." The casual passengers aboard a Windjammer can make a whole evening's entertainment around such a simple activity. Windjammer also has one slot machine on the *Polynesia* and two on the *Fantome*, but they are mostly just for show.

Music is played for the morning sails. On the *Flying Cloud*, the captain is a big classical fan, so he has classical music playing as he sails from one destination to another. Vegis chuckles, ex-plaining that the typical Windjammer passenger is not heavily into classical forms. "I mean, they come down the Caribbean to hear reggae and steel bands, the local stuff. When I go down to the Caribbean, I want to hear Caribbean music." Of course, that is one of the things that makes Windjammer cruises so personal: no one is trying to please everybody.

Passengers are free to speak out. In fact, they are encouraged to. Once you get on board, you receive a booklet called the *Wind-jammer Survival Book*. It is full of information you need to know, like what kind of currency is used on the different islands, whether or not English is spoken, and so forth. It also encourages passen-gers to give suggestions. So don't wait until the end of the cruise to say something if you have a problem. Let the crew know early on, and they will try to fix it. Vegis says, "I have seen passengers lobby for a certain island and get the captain to acquiesce and take them there. We respond to what our passengers want as much as possible."

There are no lists of rules for passengers on a Windjammer cruise. "It's not like you are an anonymous soul on a ship with

2,000 other people," Vegis explains. Windjammer vessels are so small that you make friends quickly. People will draw you in, especially veterans who have been on four or five cruises with the line—which describes many of the passengers. The crews are friendly, too. Crew members dance with passengers as part of their job. They are good at getting everyone involved.

Captains and officers of the ships tend to be British and Australian, but crew members are hired from the islands visited by the line. They are so local that when the ships stop at any given island, there is a good chance that some of the crew members are from that area. This is just one more way that Windjammer allows passengers to get a real taste of the local scene.

The line does not have dance hosts. It does not promote what Vegis terms "that kind of superficiality." Nonetheless, the crews are happy to dance. "The people of the West Indies are dancing fools. I have been to places where the entire dance floor was filled with nothing but guys." This is unlike situations in the United States where often only women are on the floor dancing. "It is not a problem getting men to dance down there. All they want to do is dance."

"We don't just have repeat passengers," boasts Vegis. "We have a cult." A spontaneous 600-member Windjammer fan club operates on Prodigy. Vegis visits the on-line site now and then to answer questions. Fans put together scrapbooks of their cruises and send them all around the country. Windjammer itself has established the Sea Dog Society, for people who have sailed on its ships a total of five weeks or more. There are over 700 members.

ITINERARY AND SEA SIGHTS

Windjammer ships sail to a different place every day. Most of the sailing is done at night, although some daytime sailing is done.

Vegis says, "We are unlike the typical cruise liner that tries to keep you on board as much as possible so you spend all your money there." The ship will arrive at the scheduled island between eight and ten o'clock in the morning, and it usually won't leave until eleven o'clock at night.

Windjammer gives total control of the itinerary to the captain. If he sails up to an island where a big ship is unloading all its passengers onto a beach, he can decide to keep on going to the next island. Windjammer's policy is to place management decisions as close to the passengers as possible so that their captains can respond quickly to their needs. The captain might also pass by an island for such reasons as finding the tides not right, making for a touchy landing. Windjammer's vessels aren't floating hotels; they are real ships, subject to nature's forces.

When booking your cruise with Windjammer, you are likely to be given a selection of islands that the captain will *probably* go to. If he pulls up to an island and doesn't like the look of things, he can move on to the next one. Or one week he will go to one island, but the next week there might be an event on a different island, so he will go there. Passengers will get a list of where they might go, a selection of ten islands or so; they can plan on hitting five of them.

SHORE EXCURSIONS

On a Windjammer cruise, you really get to experience the islands you visit. Many passengers, upon arriving in a place like St. Bart's, will rent mopeds and scatter to see the island, finding their own restaurants for dinner. Shuttle launches travel back and forth between the ship and the docks every half hour.

Sometimes the cruise line will organize with restaurants or resorts on an island and have a "jump off" night, which everyone on the island attends. "It's just kind of a big party that they have," says Vegis. In St. Bart's, for example, the ship will get in at nine or ten in the morning, and the crew will most likely arrange a party in one of the restaurants. They pay for the band, and passengers can buy drinks from the bar.

The crews of the ships mix well with the island peoples. "We've been sailing in the area forever, so we've become one of the mainstays of many islands' economies." Windjammer is the only cruise line that visits Palm Island. It bolsters the local economy. The residents love the ships' passengers and do everything they can to make them happy.

THEME AND SPECIAL-INTEREST CRUISES

Windjammer has singles-only cruises throughout the year. It had six such cruises in 1996 and seven in 1997, and it plans seven or eight for 1998. They make sure they have a balanced booking— once they fill half the ship with one sex, they stop booking that sex.

The singles cruises have been very successful. "We've been running them since 1991, and we keep planning more of them because they get more popular," says Vegis. To prove how successful they are, Vegis cites the six weddings that have resulted from people meeting on the ships. Windjammer knows that statistic is real, because it gives a free cruise to any couple that marries as a result of meeting on one of the ships. "Every once in a while, we will hear from them," says Vegis. "Like the person from Connecticut who met someone from Texas on our ship. They kept the relationship going and ended up getting married."

All the singles cruises are six days in length. Boarding is usually on Sunday, with the sailing commencing around noon on Monday.

CRUISING SEASONS

Windjammer's high season is whenever it is cold up north. Winter down in the islands is for singles. Of course, the cruises are more expensive then. The line does have off-season rates, but then everything in the islands gets more expensive.

During its high season, the line gets more requests than it can handle. During the off-season, from April to December, you can usually get a space easily. The ships are sailing only 75 to 80 percent of capacity that time of year. The rest of the year, they sail at full capacity. Prices do change with the seasons.

SPECIAL PACKAGES AND ADD-ONS

The line has what is called stowaway night (an extra night on board), for which it does charge extra. Currently, the charge is $45.

Windjammer sometimes offers special discounts, such as a discount for teachers. Windjammer gets its mailing lists from special-interest agencies, such as the National Education Association. A direct-mail piece recently went out to teachers, firefighters, police officers, and nurses. In this promotion, for every full-fare passenger, a buddy could go for half fare if the person had teaching credentials.

PRECRUISE INFORMATION

Windjammer sends out little books before you embark on your cruise, telling you what you can expect. It has a packing list, and it describes a typical day aboard a tall ship.

*N*EW AND FUTURE POSSIBILITIES

In 1998, the *Flying Cloud* will offer a singles party cruise out of the British Virgin Islands.

Windjammer has a ship under reconstruction right now in Trinidad. According to Vegis, "We plan to sail it down to Miami, at least for the first six months after its launch, just so we can go past the big cruise liners, and moon them and shoot off our canons." Apparently, Windjammer plans to do whatever it takes to make passengers on the big cruise ships hit themselves on the forehead and say, "Shoot, we could have had a Windjammer cruise!"

*W*indstar Cruises

300 Elliott Avenue West
Seattle, WA 98119
Telephone (206) 281-3535 or (800) 258-7245
On-line address: www.windstarcruises.com

"We are definitely not your mass-market cruise line" says Erik Elvejord, manager of public relations of Windstar Cruises. The line strives to offer the best in quality, but with a very laid-back atmosphere. Windstar ships cruise the Caribbean and the Mediterranean and make weekly trips to French Polynesia.

Windstar won't turn away the business of singles, but Elvejord is frank in stating that the line doesn't go out of its way to court singles on its cruise ships. Because of the way the ships are set up, they attract mostly couples. "All of our passengers, especially our alumni, have favorite itineraries," boast Elvejord, "but, universally, the most favored destination is just being on board one of our ships—anywhere in the world."

Elvejord recommends that cruise shoppers consider the all-inclusive nature of a cruise versus a resort with comparable features. Overall cruising is usually a better deal than a resort, with the added plus of visiting more destinations with greater convenience. "As far as a lot of our passengers are concerned, it's a bargain at any price."

*G*ENERAL SHIP INFORMATION

Windstar Cruises operates three four-masted schooners as an alternative to the typical cruise. These sailing ships offer luxurious voyages—unique, romantic cruises with unusual itineraries, deluxe accommodations, and five-star service. Each schooner has seventy-four cabins that include all amenities.

Windstar's three ships are the *Wind Star*, the *Wind Song*, and the *Wind Spirit*. Each holds approximately 148 passengers. The ships are virtually identical, though the color schemes are slightly different. "The ships are four-masted, modern sail cruisers," says Elvejord. When he says modern, he means just that. Everything on board is computerized, so this is not a ship where the crew has to hoist the sails. The sails are there for ambience, to be used about 60 to 80 percent of the time. The ship also has engines. Which method is used to power the ships depends on the itinerary and the weather.

Windstar ships look like sailing vessels, but they are built like cruise ships. The bottom of a Windstar ship looks a lot like a cruise vessel—it is flat. There also are stabilizers that come out sixteen meters on either side, to stabilize the ship in rough seas. When the sails are up, the ship operates on a computerized ballast system located down in the hull. If the wind kicks up and the ship starts to heel, the sensors on the ship measure the exact degree of heel. When it reaches more than six degrees, the water ballast system shifts water from side to side, keeping the ship within a range of no more than six degrees of motion. In terms of the ride, a Windstar ship is designed like a cruise ship, which rides very smoothly.

DESTINATIONS, LENGTH OF CRUISES, DEPARTURE PORTS

The *Wind Star* and *Wind Spirit* sail to the Caribbean, the Mediterranean, both the French and Italian Rivieras, and the Greek islands. These two ships winter in the Caribbean, then reposition to Europe at the end of March or early April, returning at the end of October. The European cruises depart from Nice, France, Athens, or Istanbul.

The *Wind Song* will make weekly cruises of French Polynesia through November 1997, and then it will begin its first season in Costa Rica. In late March, it will reposition to Rome, to sail the Amalfi coast through the summer.

Most of the line's cruises are one-week vacations. A few are longer, when the ships are making their transatlantic repositioning voyages. The general itineraries in the Caribbean, Polynesia, Costa Rica, the Greek islands, and the Rivieras are one-week cruises.

"I think the Pacific tropics—either Costa Rica or Polynesia—is a great destination, particularly for West Coast travelers," says Elvejord, "because it is easier to get there. It's a shorter distance if you live in Los Angeles." For East Coast residents, Elvejord recommends Windstar as a great way to experience the Caribbean, for those who like sun and sea and beaches with a little culture mixed in here and there.

ACCOMMODATIONS FOR SINGLES

Because of the intimacy of Windstar ships, the line does not provide packages or services for singles. There is no dance host or escort program or other special items that might attract singles, except the destinations and the casual atmosphere. For single travelers, it is most cost-effective to find another single to share your cabin.

PASSENGER INFORMATION

In general, Windstar hosts couples on its cruises: married couples, people who are just friends, couples who live in widely separate areas of the country. Singles tend to be in groups of friends traveling together. Sometimes mother-and-daughter pairs are on board. "Occasionally, you will see single people in a cabin not traveling with anyone else, but to be honest, it's quite rare," says Elvejord.

A good majority of the people who sail with Windstar are health-conscious. That does not necessarily mean they are super athletic. They are not all jocks, but they do some sort of regular exercise and enjoy being active. "A lot of people fear that if they get on one of our ships they will be surrounded by all these athletic young people," says Elvejord. "That is not the case."

ONBOARD LIFE

Windstar ships are small and very intimate. The maximum of 148 passengers sail with an attentive crew of eighty-eight per vessel. On board, the atmosphere is very laid back. There are no formal nights, no shows, no revues, no midnight buffets. The cruises are designed to be very relaxed and very casual, yet they are also very upscale, with signature cuisine and high-quality service. Windstar is for people who don't want a cruise with a Las Vegas show.

Once you are on board, take the opportunity to chat with your hosts and to read your daily program, which is placed in your stateroom each evening. Windstar offers optional shore excursions, all coordinated by the company through local tour operators. When you board the ship you will receive a complete list of excursions. The staff usually asks that you sign up a day in advance so they can count the numbers of attendees.

Unusual shore excursions and complimentary water sports are available at each of the Windstar destinations. You will get briefing sheets on each port. The hosts know about the best restaurants, the best hikes, the best stores, and anything else you want to know about your destinations. They are always happy to give you some advice, telling you how long certain activities might take, for instance. You can get anything and everything you need in terms of information. If all you want to do is find a beach where you can lay out by yourself, the hosts can tell you where the sandy beaches are, give you directions for reaching them, and tell you how long it will take to get there. If you want a beach with shells, they can point you to a beach with shells.

If you want to shop, say, to buy a black pearl, they can tell you the best places to buy a black pearl. That sort of request is usually well taken care of on the ship. There is no question they can't answer—or find the answer to relatively quickly.

Most members of the crew know each port well and are always happy to point out the local hot spots to meet and mingle. Don't be surprised if many of the crew know you by name the first day and the pool bartender remembers your drink preference the second time you order. That experience is exactly what Windstar is all about.

Windstar's crew-to-passenger ratio tells you something of what to expect on board. The ships sail with a staff of eighty-eight for 148 passengers. With that ratio, the level of service is unmatched, and it lends itself to a real sense of camaraderie between passengers and crew. At the end of a Windstar cruise, it is not surprising to see the crew and passengers exchanging fond good-byes—and even addresses to stay in touch.

Windstar's officers are mainly British and Dutch. The intimate size of the ship really gives you a chance to interact with the crew. The officers always enjoy sharing stories of the high seas, and the bridge is open twenty-four hours a day. Stop by anytime to find out more about sailing and navigation.

The service staff—the cabin stewards, kitchen, and dining room people—are primarily Indonesian and Philippino. They take pride in providing for every detail so that your desires are quickly fulfilled—and always with a smile.

The passengers aboard a Windstar ship dine in casual elegance. Dress is very informal. Men don't need a tie at dinner. The only thing Windstar asks is that you not wear jeans. Casual khaki pants and a button-up or polo shirt for men is okay. For women, pantsuits or sundresses are appropriate. Packing is certainly a lot lighter when you sail with Windstar, because you don't have to bring a formal dress or a suit and tie.

"Casual" is open to interpretation. "I've seen people wear a tie to dinner, and I've seen people wear what I would consider less than casual," says Elvejord, "but they were allowed to eat."

There is one seating at dinner, and it is anytime between 7:30 and 9:30. Just show up and you are seated, as in a restaurant. Seating is therefore open; there are no assigned seats. You can choose an intimate window table for two, or you can join a group of newfound friends. "You can sit anywhere you like," says Elvejord. The only restriction is if you want to reserve a big table for a group of eight or more. In that case, the dining room manager would like you to reserve the space a day ahead of time.

The captain always hosts a table for dinner one or two nights out of the cruise, and often other officers will join passengers for dinner.

You can also have dinner sent to your room. There is twenty-four-hour room service, which offers passengers another flexible alternative.

On deck, shorts and T-shirts are the order of the day. There is a lot of swimming and snorkeling and sightseeing on these cruises, so you are not required to dress up during the day. "Men especially like the casual dress code," says Elvejord.

People also select Windstar ships because they can do their own thing. In the evening, there is a small entertainment group on board. You will always find some people in the lounge listening to music or dancing. Others will check out a video. Every cabin has a VCR, and movies are run on the closed-circuit television system. You can also check out any of the large selection of videos and CDs to enjoy in the comfort of your stateroom. Windstar has 500 videos and CDs in its library.

If the ship is in port at evening, many people go ashore to have drinks and dance, depending upon the locale. In Polynesia, public places usually shut down ashore after dark, which is quite different than in Europe, where places stay open until midnight or one o'clock. In Bora Bora, when it gets dark you've got the stars and the moon and that's pretty much it.

Evenings ashore can be casual, depending on the destination. Europe tends to be a bit more formal than the Caribbean or elsewhere in the tropics. You will see men wearing a jacket in Europe more often than in Polynesia. Men who want to get into a casino on the French Riviera or Monte Carlo won't be able to without a jacket. So they should be sure to bring a jacket for some of the establishments ashore. Women can generally get away with more than men can, fashionwise.

BEST BETS FOR MEETING PEOPLE

Just because Windstar does not have many singles aboard does not mean single passengers will feel ostracized. "It's amazing how quickly people will pick up on the fact that you are in a cabin by yourself," says Elvejord. People will often include you simply because you are alone. With just 148 passengers, it will be only a matter days before you know everybody on the ship, where they come from, and what their line of work is.

The optional shore excursions and Windstar's complimentary water sports program are great ways to get to know your fellow travelers naturally, in situations in which you have the common interest of the shared activities.

ᏚHORE EXCURSIONS

Windstar's shore excursions range from parasailing to shark snorkeling to island, history, and cultural tours.

Yes, shark snorkeling. The sharks in question are black-tipped reef sharks, which have been trained and are conditioned by handlers. This is an interesting and exciting shore excursion, and it is not as dangerous as it sounds. It is a little eerie at times to be face to face with a shark, which can be three to six feet long but is not dangerous. The trainers feed them, and snorkeling passengers really just observe. You can also feed stingrays if you want. The guide will place food in your hand and you simply hold it out, as if you were feeding a horse an apple. The shark and stingray excursion attracts a range of ages, but individual participation depends on a certain comfort level with both water and sea life. This is one of Windstar's more adventurous and unique excursions.

Those thinking about a Windstar cruise should consider the fact that the primary activities will be water sports, sightseeing, and beachcombing, particularly in the tropics. These are attractive components of what the cruise line has to offer.

The line's unusual variety of shore excursions are enjoyed by both young and old, active and inactive. "I've seen all types of people on the *Stars and Stripes* mini regatta sailing excursion. Everybody has a blast," says Elvejord. They do have some of the standard shore excursions, but for the most part Windstar's excursion are far from run-of-the-mill. For example, four wheel driving in Bora Bora may not appeal to everybody, especially those who will feel the bumps more, but people still have a lot of fun heading up into the mountains there.

Many passengers like to water-ski. This is part of the complimentary water sports program offered by the ships. If you are not especially gifted at any of the offered activities, you can try anyway. You can have fun, and nobody will laugh at you. It actually creates a feeling of camaraderie, of being aboard with a select group, almost like your own private yacht party.

Some less adventurous shore excursions highlight regional cultures and histories, such as the French and Artistic Tour on St. Martin and the Rhodes Town and Castle Tour in Greece. There are also cultural tours and wine tasting tours. In the Caribbean, one of the excursions allows you to sail the *Stars and Stripes* racing yacht, which is a lot of fun.

PERSONAL SAFETY

When you get on your cruise ship, don't leave your common sense back at home. If you are going to leave the ship at night, Elvejord recommends that you go with somebody. "It's just common sense. I think it is good to explore in numbers." As well, it is always a good idea to know when your ship is scheduled to depart.

Polynesia is an area where no one will really bother you, however at night on some of the islands there are no lights. That can be a startling surprise to some visitors.

THEME AND SPECIAL-INTEREST CRUISES

Windstar offers food-and-wine theme cruises. Celebrity chef Graham Kerr will be on board, as will Matthew Kinney, the great new chef out of New York, and Joe Cochran, the chef from the Mission Inn in California. Nick Stellino, from the PBS show *Cucina Amore*, will be on board to demonstrate recipes from Windstar's own kitchen. Marsha Mondavi of Robert Mondavi Winery will conduct onboard wine tastings.

CRUISING SEASONS

You might think that summertime would be high season for Windstar cruising, because the universities are out, teachers are off, and so forth, but summer doesn't impact Windstar in the same way it does other cruise lines. Since Windstar operates year-round in Polynesia, there isn't any one time of year that attracts more singles than others.

PRECRUISE INFORMATION

A mistake people can make when considering a Windstar cruise is to misunderstand this cruise line's vision. If you are looking for an endless party with lots of people and a very festive atmosphere, then you might be disappointed by a Windstar cruise. You will meet a lot of people, but you won't find any raging party mood. If you are looking for revelry and action, you might want to consider another cruise line.

If, on the other hand, you are looking for a great vacation and you don't want to be hassled, then come to Windstar first.

On these ships, *you* decide what you want to do, who you want to talk to, and when you want to stay in your cabin. The waiters and the service crew will certainly ask if they can get you something, and an officer might stop and say hello, but if you just want to hang out and read a book all day in some quiet corner, that is exactly what you can do. The more social types will meet people and talk, but in a less hassling way than on other cruises.

As Elvejord advises, "We say this to singles or anybody: If you want to get dressed up, if you want to wear a tux or an evening gown, and you love the idea of seeing a show and dancing all night long, then Windstar is not for you. On the other hand, if you want to put on a pair of shorts and relax, then we may be the perfect vacation experience for you." When you're thinking about a Windstar cruise, consider the following questions: What are you looking for in the cruise ship experience? What destinations do you have in mind? Do you enjoy water sports? Anyone who enjoys beautiful settings and the pampering of an attentive yet unobtrusive staff will enjoy a Windstar cruise.

Windstar Cruises always recommends that you book through a travel agent. Many agents specialize in cruising, and they can work out a perfect vacation from beginning to end at a price that is right for you.

$\mathcal{W}$orld Explorer Cruises

555 Montgomery Street, Suite 1400
San Francisco, CA 94111
Telephone (415) 393-1565 or (800) 854-3835

A veteran in the Alaska cruise market, World Explorer is known for its informality and educational focus as well as for offering more ports of call and more time in each port than any other Alaska cruise line. It takes passengers to ports not often visited by other cruise ships. Nonetheless, its fourteen-day cruises are offered at the same price as many other lines' seven-day Alaska cruises. It makes eight voyages a year in Alaska and two in Latin America.

"And we're very affordable," adds Dennis M. Myrick, vice president of World Explorer Cruises.

$\mathcal{G}$ENERAL SHIP INFORMATION

World Explorer Cruises has one ship, the SS *Universe Explorer*, known for its uncommon route in Alaska. The ship holds 739 people—not the usual megaship, but then its cruises are not routine either.

Other cruise lines don't offer any packages similar to World Explorer's two-week passage, because costwise it would be ineffective. With their brand-new ships that hold 2,000 people, other lines have to turn their passenger rosters over every seven days. "It's like a Whitman's Sampler on those seven-day cruises," says Myrick. "Passengers are lucky if they visit two or three ports for maybe five or six hours each, hit a gift shop, and get back on board. Those lines don't even really care if you get off the ship or not." World Explorer cares. Crew members want you to get off the ship—they want you to learn about totem poles, how they're made, how to read them, and the significance of totem poles in the history of the Chilkat Indians and the Eskimo culture. They feel that such things are an important part of visiting Alaska.

DESTINATIONS, LENGTH OF CRUISES, DEPARTURE PORTS

During World Explorer's sixteen-week season, it offers eight two-week voyages. It also now offers two fourteen-day voyages, in late December through January, in the western Caribbean and Latin America. "We are unique in having the fourteen-day voyages," says Myrick.

The Alaska cruises go up the inside passage, across Glacier Bay to Valdez, then even farther over to the Seward and Anchorage areas. This route is a World Explorer exclusive. Moreover, World Explorer visits more ports in Alaska than any other cruise line. It also spends more time in port than any other Alaska cruise line. The ships average nine hours of port time in every port they visit.

December 28, 1997, will inaugurate World Explorer's first fourteen-day voyage to the western Caribbean, Mexico's Yucatan peninsula, and Central and South America. Again, it will take an uncommon route. The line likes to specialize in ports of call that most cruise lines don't visit, not only in Alaska, but in this new area as well.

Ships will go to Honduras and Costa Rica, with two days and one night in Costa Rica, so passengers will have a real chance to get off the ship and go to the interior. Costa Rica has two distinctly different regions: the volcanic region and the jungle region. "Costa Rica is a beautiful country," says Myrick. "Over 32 percent of it is protected habitats." (In comparison, the U.S. is about 10 percent protected.)

The *Universe Explorer* will go on to Panama from Costa Rica, then on to Colombia, Jamaica, and Calica. "These cruises will be less expensive than cruises in Alaska," explains Myrick, "because the distances are such that we will not burn as much fuel as on the Alaska cruises, which cover well over 3,000 miles in two weeks."

*A*CCOMMODATIONS FOR SINGLES

World Explorer does not have a share program, but it does offer a very good single supplement of 30 percent, so it is not that expensive to travel by yourself. For example, if the cabin accommodation normally sells for $1,000 per person, based on double occupancy, and two people are in the cabin, then of course that cabin will sell for $2,000. But if there is only one person in the cabin, then the price is $1,300. Instead of paying the full 100 percent of the empty berth, you pay only 30 percent. That is one of the many ways in which World Explorer encourages singles to sail on its cruises.

PASSENGER INFORMATION

Alaska seems to attract an older crowd; age fifty-plus is usual for World Explorer. There are also families on board most voyages because it is a summer program, which is the time when the kids are out of school. Primarily, though, it is a fifty-plus crowd.

The World Explorer crowd is made up of intellectual, literary people who are really interested in the destination; these are people who want to be actively involved in their vacation. If you are one of those people, you will be amply rewarded with the culture, the history, the people, the folkways, the morays, the fauna, the flora, the beauty, and the scenery of Alaska. "If you want to just sit in your cabin or on deck reading a novel, you shouldn't even go," warns Myrick.

ONBOARD LIFE

There is no glitz here, no Broadway shows, no gambling. The *Universe Explorer* attracts passengers who want to experience the Last Frontier by spending fourteen days immersed in its art, history, and culture. Keep in mind that things are very casual and informal. There is no need to dress up every night for dinner. The ship doesn't have a casino aboard. There are no jugglers, comedians, or cancan girls.

World Explorer generally has four or five experts on every voyage, which might include anthropologists, archeologists, oceanographers, historians, and others. They conduct informal presentations prior to arrival in each port, so that when guests do leave the ship for those nine hours they have a better understanding of what there is to see and do in each port.

You should let the cruise director know if you are traveling by yourself. The cruise director will make sure you won't feel alone. The ship's very size makes the entire experience intimate, so you are soon bound to feel part of a family.

Also, tell the maitre d' that you are by yourself. You might be able to sit with other people traveling by themselves. You will want to hook up with one or more companions, so make it known that you are traveling solo, and the quicker the better. People will start gravitating towards you. It also probably wouldn't hurt for you to attend activities offered on board.

In light of World Explorer's emphasis on destinations, it may surprise you to learn that dance hosts are on board all its voyages. The line has offered this service for several years now, and it goes over very well with women passengers. World Explorer has every intention of continuing the service. "I don't need to mention that we match our host's intellect to what we assume to be the intellect of our passengers, which is pretty high," say Myrick. The hosts can usually be found in the Commodore Lounge.

In any case, single women passengers will definitely not feel uncomfortable being by themselves. World Explorer has such a community atmosphere on board its two-week voyage that any and all are welcome. Any single passenger, male or female, certainly will not feel awkward about traveling without a companion.

The *Universe Explorer* is a midsize ship, so you get to know the other people on board fairly well. You are with them for two weeks. You are in the lectures together and on shore excursions together. There are plenty of opportunities for interaction. So it doesn't really matter whether you are traveling as a couple or by yourself.

Though you are sent a booklet of available tours before you sail, you book these tours after boarding. Two orientations presented during the voyage give much more complete information, hints, and suggestions about the tours. The line recommends that you wait to book until you have heard the onboard briefings.

In Alaska, the ship will typically arrive at its destination at 7:00 A.M. Passengers are asked to be back by 8:00 or 9:00 P.M., so the ship can sail at 10:00. During the summer, it is daylight almost until midnight, so while in port, you can be out on a tour at 6:00 or 7:00 at night and still get back in time for dinner on the ship. Or you might opt to take a tour early in the day and do some private exploring of the port on your own in the afternoon and evening. The extended day in Alaska really multiplies touring possibilities.

On the Alaska cruise, the only time the passengers spend a little time at sea is when the ship crosses the Gulf of Alaska and heads towards Valdez after leaving Glacier Bay. You will be at sea for about twenty-four hours. On board, you can attend lectures and video presentations on Alaska. There is plenty of activity on board during the rare day at sea.

The clothes you pack for this cruise should definitely be casual. The weather can get chilly in the evening in Alaska, so you might consider the layered look. For instance, you might want to add a windbreaker or a sweater to your outfit, depending on the weather conditions.

◈HORE EXCURSIONS

Nine hours in each port assures passengers that there is plenty of time to take one of World Explorer's organized shore excursions and still have plenty of time to explore the port on their own.

World Explorer offers more than fifty optional shore tours, ranging in interest and appeal for singles as well as couples. There are plenty of activities for those who enjoy a bit of adventure: river rafting, gold panning (of course), some pretty exotic "flight-seeing" trips with helicopters and float planes, and nature and wildlife tours. There is lots that will appeal to people traveling by themselves.

$\mathcal{P}$ERSONAL SAFETY

World Explorer does not suggest that anybody go alone into the back country of any destination. The cruise destinations are remote. There is wildlife back there. All the line's tours are escorted by experienced guides, and you are advised to take an organized tour. You should never be by yourself on shore, whether in Alaska, South America, Florida, or California. Stay with the group or with a group of friends.

$\mathcal{T}$HEME AND SPECIAL-INTEREST CRUISES

The world cruise offered by this line is again quite different from other cruises. When a World Explorer ship pulls into a port, it stays there from three to six days. You get to go into the interior of the countries and really experience the culture. "It is absolutely fascinating," claims Myrick. "The cruise lasts 100 days, and the ports we visit are not your typical glitz and glitter." This is a chance for passengers to really see a part of the world they would never see on their own; for example, the ship spends three days each in Kenya, Madras, India, and South Africa.

World Explorer shares a vessel with a Hong Kong–based concern for this venture. It offers two 100-day voyages around the world, primarily for students, although it has taken a limited number of adults on these world voyages. Adults who take this around-the-world cruise are people looking for an inexpensive world voyage who also want to get to know the people, the places, and the history of each port they visit.

Up to 100 adults are allowed on the student world cruises. This is one of the best deals around, especially for anyone who has a lot of discretionary time. Prices for this cruise are based on double occupancy.

A voyage left September 1997 out of Vancouver. It went to Kobe, Japan, to Shanghai, to Hong Kong, Ho Chi Minh City in Vietnam, Madras in India, Port Said in Egypt, to Israel, Istanbul in Turkey, to Greece, and then to Casablanca in Morocco before returning to Florida. "How many people have a chance to go to Egypt, India, Vietnam, Turkey, and Greece?" Myrick asks. The itinerary varies a little on every voyage. The next voyage, for example, will also go to Brazil, Venezuela, South Africa, Kenya, and the Philippines.

CRUISING SEASONS

World Explorer's Alaska season is from mid-May until mid-September. The western Caribbean and Latin America voyages sail in late December through January.

PRECRUISE INFORMATION

You will get a description of World Explorer's optional shore excursions a month to six weeks before sailing. When sending out your cruise tickets, World Explorer encloses a shore excursion booklet, giving you a full month to review what will be offered once you board the ship. This allows you to plan what you might want to do.

CHAPTER 16

*W*hat Cruising Is Really Like

We knew from our many single female friends that women were definitely interested in considering cruise vacations, but we wondered about how single men felt. Were they thinking about it, and if they had cruised, how did they like it? What man would tell us what it was really like? We pondered the question until we met Lee Burke, bachelor and veteran Windjammer cruiser who agreed to share reminiscences of his voyages on Windjammer Barefoot Cruises:

Passengers begin to arrive on the pier in Phillipsburg, in St. Maarten. Some of us are two hours early due to plane arrival times. Everyone greets newcomers as they arrive. Introductions are made. By common agreement, we decide to go to a local bar and have a few drinks. The normal questions are asked: What's your name? Where are you from? What do you do? Is this your first time Windjamming? For the majority, this is their first cruise with the line. They have heard about the cruises from friends.

Soon, we (there may be from six to twenty-five of us) decide to take a stroll about the town. It is Sunday, so Phillipsburg is all but deserted. The shops are closed. We end up on the pier again, where we meet more of our fellow Windjammers. Everyone is in a good mood. We're going to have the best of times. Some of us take a quick swim with our new friends. Some hang out at the pier to check out the new arrivals or try to impress someone they've just met and like. Some continue to walk the town.

Our ship is the *Polynesia*. She holds 126 passengers, all of whom board at 5:00 P.M. Well, almost all. A later flight arriving that night will bring in another ten to fifteen people. Launches take us out to the ship. As we approach and board, I hear a lot of aahs and oohs. Most people have seen something like the *Polynesia* only in those old Errol Flynn movies.

Once aboard, we are given free—and rather strong—rum swizzles. Then we check in. This takes about half an hour. As each of us finish, we go to our cabins and look them over. No one stays below too long, however. We soon all reassemble on the top deck to view the harbor and continue to get to know our fellow passengers. Already I can see some people pairing up. We buy more drinks, which seem to be particularly strong that first night.

Dinner is called. It's a buffet, which is excellent. After eating, we refresh our drinks and go back onto the top deck.

This is where the real mixing starts. Everyone is looking around, checking out everyone else, now that most of us are aboard. The band is setting up by then. The ship always has a reggae band the first night. Everyone gets a chance to say hello to everyone else, but some are steering toward certain people who interest them.

The passengers are of all ages, sizes, shapes, and personalities, so there is a lot of variety. People tend to make friends with others of the same sex first. That goes for males and females. Of course, the men aren't as interested in forming friendships with other men as they are with women. The groups intermingle. We make small talk, find out who is interesting and whether they seem interested. We merge and mingle some more. Sometimes two people hit it off right away and mingle no more.

The band starts to play. Strange as it seems, no one dances during the first song. Some brave soul always has to ask another to dance and get out there and be the first, then others will follow. I have done that at times, because I've learned that's just the way it is. After all, we've just met, and people are still shy.

By the middle of the next song, a whole bunch of people are dancing. With the next song, even more are dancing. I can see the smiles and hear laughter from both those dancing and those who are still watching. The cool part is that the people dancing are not only the beautiful people but also the shy types and even the not so beautiful. It must be the atmosphere—and the drinks.

Gradually, everyone starts to realize that the songs are somewhere in the area of forty-five minutes long! That's a lot of dancing. I need to go for another drink. I offer to buy one for the person I danced with. We do some more of the small talk thing, to find out more about each other, and then we mingle and merge some more. This is called Heat and Seek.

I find those men friends I made earlier and say hi. I get another drink and move around the deck. That first night is mostly about meeting different people. It's fun. Both men and women dance a lot and joke and laugh—and just plain have fun. Some members of the group may have already matched up. Usually only a few do, maybe ten couples. I have paired up the first night, and it is a mixed blessing. It depends on who you meet.

About a fourth of the passengers stay up very late, say till 3:00 A.M., and talk about whatever meets their fancy. By that time, some are lying on a mat on the top deck. This late group is usually mixed, males and females. It is, by all accounts, a very good night.

That first night is where most people lay the groundwork for the next few days of the cruise. On Monday, the ship sets sail. Everyone lays out on the deck for some sun. There are mats all over. People I met, danced with, and talked to the night before are the ones I lie down next to. The chatting starts again.

Monday is an all-day sail. The feeling of sailing is excellent. Everyone notices how nice it is. Everyone is in a wonderful mood. The atmosphere is great. It's easy to converse with people, tell jokes, kid around, and just plain laugh. People start forming friendships with both women and men. The women sometimes gather in little groups to talk to each other, and so do the men. It is a day for establishing friendships.

That night, the ship provides some activities, like crab races, where little crabs have to cross a circle. Little entertainments. People continue to develop their friendships. If the ship is going to arrive in St. Bart's, for example, people are asking what there is to do on the island. There are always a few like me who have been to the island before. We answer questions for others. The next thing, groups are forming with plans to tour the island and do things like beaching, shopping, and just exploring the island. This second night is when both men and women find the people, or person, they like. If you are lucky, you will fall in with someone special for the rest of the cruise.

There is more dancing, to CDs this time, down by the bar. The music echoes up to the top deck, where some of us like to dance and talk at the same time. It is hard to describe that second night. For some, it is the best night. Strong friendships are made.

Most people stay up late into the night doing the usual things: laughing, smiling, dancing, drinking. We don't drink *too* much, since we don't want to act like jerks. This is called "casual drinking," with lots of talking, asking each other the questions that new friends do. It is a great night.

The third day, Tuesday, we arrive on St. Bart's. Our little groups get together and have our adventures on the island. I like to walk around the town of Gustovia and show my new friends what a beautiful town it is. Then I rent a mokie, which is an oversized golf cart, and we go off to the beach. I always go to Saline Beach, which is very French and one of the island's unofficial clothes-optional beaches. Governors Beach is clothes-optional too, and I like that one as well. Saline doesn't have refreshment stands, so there are no drinks or food. But I am prepared. I've packed a portable cooler, and I've stopped at the grocery store by the airport on St. Maarten and bought wine and sodas, cheese, ice, a meat spread, French bread, and some snacks.

At the beach, there are about four to six of us, half male and half female. We have a blast. Most of my fellow passengers have never been to a French beach and are amazed. The water is perfect, the sand is great, and the views are incredible.

After a few hours on the beach, we travel the island and see some great scenic coves and beaches, which are really amazing. That is the time for cameras. We may travel up a driveway in hopes that the person who owns the beautiful home at the top is not at home. That way, we can check the outside and, of course, look at the great view from the cliff. These homes cost in the millions or at least half a million. We wonder if a movie star owns it.

Later, we head back to the ship with some newly purchased French wine. Everyone was asked to pick up a bottle for a wine-and-cheese get-together at 5:00. As we share our bounty and consume the cheese, we all describe the great day we have had.

After the wine, it's shower time. Later that night, a band plays for us at the L'Select in St. Bart's.

I have been on Windjammer cruises where just being good friends was as perfect as any romance. A romance is something special, yes, but a friendship tends to last. I love them both. I have found some great women friends, and I have had some great romances. I have also found some great male friendships that are still going to this day.

Windjammer attracts a mixed bag of singles. The cool part about Windjamming as a single is that no one is left out in the cold. The first Windjammer cruise I had was the best vacation I'd ever experienced. I have been on the big cruise ships, and I love them, too. I've also gone to resorts, and I like them. Windjamming took my breath away. It still does. Before my first Windjammer cruise, the key to a great vacation was having a relationship with someone of the opposite sex. The closer the better. It is still very important, mind you, but it is no longer the only way to have a fantastic time.

On my first Windjammer cruise, in April 1994, I did not have a romance with anyone. It took me a month to figure out why it was the best vacation ever. My friends couldn't understand, because I couldn't tell them why it was so good. I wrote my trip report and read it again a couple of weeks later. I finally figured it out. It was right in front of me. I enjoyed my vacation because *I had a great time*. I laughed a lot. I smiled constantly. I danced all the time. I made women friends—good friends—and made good male friends, too.

I remember sleeping on the deck one night with a group of about eight. We had helped raise the sails at around eleven o'clock that night. We drank champagne as the ship slid out into the dark sea. "Amazing Grace" was playing, which always happens with the raising of the sails, and the captain shut off the ship's lights on the top deck. As the song played, we looked up at the millions and millions of stars. After an hour of camaraderie, some of us fell asleep. Some of us stayed awake, silent now. The wind was light, the air was warm, the moon was a quarter full. I looked up at the sea of stars: so bright, so clear, so close. The ship rocked lightly, causing the stars to seem to rock. The Milky Way was sharply visible. I was a little boy again, with the wonder of a child's innocence. It took me a long time to fall asleep. All of us, men and women alike, felt the magic that night.

It's easy for men to meet women and for women to meet men on a Windjammer cruise. It doesn't even have to be a singles cruise. It can be a routine mixed couples and singles sailing. The ship doesn't hold 800 or 2,500 passengers. You do not meet someone for a minute, then never see that person again. There is no rush. On a Windjammer, you will see that person again within minutes, certainly in less than an hour. You can just say hi and have small talk, go on your way, and meet up again later, again saying hi and increasing the small talk to something more. Buy her a drink. Tell a story. Talk about the island you will see tomorrow. Ask what her plans are. Maybe even get her to agree to hang out with you the next day. You can meet by just going on a taxi tour that travels around the islands showing the sights. A taxi holds up to ten people on many of the islands. That's another great chance to get to know other people. Later that night on the ship, you have more to talk about and to laugh over. The friendship has started.

The two best ships for singles are the *Polynesia* and the *Flying Cloud*. The *Polynesia* is the one that sings to singles. She visits the best islands for singles to have fun on. With only 126 passengers, you get to know a lot of them quickly. Being outgoing helps, especially the first night or two. Even the ones who are hesitant find that they make friends rather easily. For every outgoing person, there is a shy person. The shy mix with the shy and find that they are now outgoing. Being handsome or pretty helps, but it does not control the final outcome of the cruise. As I said before, when people become friends, looks are less important.

On that first Windjammer cruise, I went alone and was assigned a cabin mate. He was fifty years old and a power company lineman from Ohio. It was a cold winter that year, and he had worked long and hard in extremely cold weather repairing storm-downed lines. It was one of the worst winters he'd ever experienced on the job. He was also still grieving for a son who had died a year before. His wife had left him. He'd just kicked his daughter out of the house. He loved her, but she was addicted to drugs and was stealing and lying. He felt like a failure as a father, a husband, a human being.

He was a nice guy, but life just was not nice to him. He was depressed. The first two days of the cruise, he stayed in the cabin a lot, which hardly anyone does. He thought about his life and his troubles. I tried my best to get him to come up and join us. He tried, but it just did not work. I felt for him, but I couldn't make him have a good time. The third night, a band came aboard, and we all danced. I noticed he was dancing with someone. From that night on, he was always on deck, laughing and smiling. He talked to people, joked, and joined in the activities. He had fun.

The last night on the ship, he told me he'd never expected to have a good time, didn't want to have a good time. He hadn't even wanted to go on the cruise, but friends talked him into it. From the moment he asked that lady to dance, things changed. He smiled for the first time since his son died. He was sad when the cruise was over, but no one could take away what he had gained. He saw there was a chance he could still have his life back. I like to say the magic caught him. That lady who danced with him started the magic. She didn't know it, but she helped a man heal. It is magic—human magic, no doubt about it. That's what happens on Windjammer cruises.

$\mathcal{B}$est Bets

When you finally make that big decision to take a cruise, you will face an even bigger decision—how to go about finding the best deal. The literature out there is overwhelming. Some say you should book early to try for that early-bird discount, while others tell you to wait until the last possible minute, for that spur-of-the-moment discount. Where do you go for these discounts, which agencies and ads really offer true value, and how can you tell the difference? We hope this chapter gives you some insight into the dizzying world of discounts, price-slashing, first- and last-moment bargains, and travel clubs. That way you can always be sure to get the best bet.

$\mathcal{C}$RUISE TIPS FROM A PROFESSIONAL

We interviewed Michael Grossman, marketing director of Cruises of Distinction, to learn how you can cruise in style and save money. Cruises of Distinction is a mail-order company that sells cruises through catalogs all over the United States. The company is also a discounter. Cruises of Distinction catalogs are distributed free. To obtain one, call (800) 634-3445.

The first thing we asked was how Cruises of Distinction is different from Spur of the Moment, a cruise consolidator. He told us that Spur of the Moment concentrates, by its design or by its name, on last-minute cruises. At the time the company was formed, that was the way to get the best discounts. But that has changed in the last couple of years. The cruise lines themselves have introduced programs intended to give megadiscounts.

Following, in Mr. Grossman's own words, are more tips we picked up during our interview:

Book Early

Most of the reputable cruise brokers or cruise discounters offer good guaranteed prices, called price protections. If the cruise line drops the price after somebody books, the broker will reduce the price to the new lower price, just as long as the cruise line will, of course, pass the lower price on to the broker, which they will almost always do. Once in a rare while the cruise lines say no, booking only on a new offer, but that's not very often. The point is that if you book early, you will get the best cabin selection and location and you're assured, of course, of getting on the ship. If someone is giving you the price protection for the lowest price available, you're going to get the best price as well. So all the advantages are in booking early.

Most of the cruise lines have come out with a discount program. Royal Caribbean Cruise Lines started it about two years ago. They all have different names for it: Love Boat Savers for Princess; Breakthrough Pricing for Royal Caribbean; Power America; and so on. Basically what they'll do is take a ship that has the capacity of say 1,000, and they'll determine that the first 200 cabins are going to get sold at the lowest price.

If selling looks like it's going very well, the price may rise slightly after the first 200 cabins get sold, or it may stay the same. But they guarantee they won't go below the cost of the first 200, and in Royal Caribbean's case, there are a fair number of instances where they keep raising the prices as they get close to sailing, rather than the reverse.

This happens as the demand picks up, so the people who book early are rewarded with the lower price. The bottom line is that there is no great virtue in booking at the last minute anymore.

Three or four years ago, we used to tell everyone to hold off, to wait until the last minute. We're going out of our way these days to tell people that waiting is not in their best interests, because we don't think it is.

The better deals aren't coming along at the last minute anymore. The lines have gotten a lot more sophisticated in recent years in terms of predicting their inventory and predicting how many passengers they'll go out with. They therefore promote discounts as they think they're going to need them much earlier in the game than they used to.

The farther away you go, the longer the lead time seems to be. In other words, if you're going to the Caribbean for a week, then booking three or four months out ought to be, under normal circumstances, plenty of time. If you're going to Asia, however, you'd probably want to book six to nine months out. The farther away the destination, the more in advance people will plan for such a major trip, so they book well ahead of time.

Cruise Booking Companies vs. Travel Agents

Whether you go through your travel agent or through a company like Cruises of Distinction, the end result is that you walk out with a cruise.

The difference for the large cruise-only retailers that are national in scope, like ourselves, is that in some cases (but not all),

our volume is such that we have an awful lot of additional good-
ies. For example, certain cruise lines give a very small number of
select agents around the country very special, unadvertised cruises.
Our company certainly would get those.

Also consider that the typical local travel agency sells a very
wide variety of products. They're not booking hundreds of cruises
all day long, so they don't know every single cruise product—they
don't know every ship, they don't get last-minute feedback. We've
put a lot of energy and time into statistically reviewing what people
tell us about the cruises they've taken, and we've computerized
the results for any ship that you can think of in terms of about five
major categories, from food quality to cabin cleanliness.

If you're using a local agent who is booking one or two cruises
a week and a problem arises, the local agent doesn't really have
the ability to pick up the telephone and call the senior cruise line
official. Even if local agents could do that, they don't have the
juice that a company like ours, which does high volume, has. So,
Cruises of Distinction's service is at least as good or perhaps better because of the knowledge and the experience. And there are
so many deals on the marketplace these days.

Another point to consider is that there are lots of regional
deals, good only for the state of Kansas, for instance, or for the
city of Omaha. Some private deals are given only to large-volume
producers. There are one-day sales as well as a whole slew of new
deals being introduced. Our organization is on top of those kinds
of deals. For example, we would know that Cruise Line A is giving the business class upgrade for a week or that Cruise Line B is
giving a three-category upgrade. We can pass that knowledge on
to our clients.

In the end, it's a matter of preference. There are very good
local agents and there are very bad local agents. There are people

who don't like to deal by direct mail, although that number seems to be diminishing.

Single Supplements

Many lines offer share programs, and they typically work as follows. You give the lines certain parameters: sex, age, smoking or nonsmoking, that sort of thing. Many of the lines will say that if they can't match you up, they will give you the matched price. You'll just have the cabin to yourself. You won't have to pay the single supplement. Cruises of Distinction doesn't put people together, but we go to the cruise lines, who do put people together.

Instant Notice

We have a program called Instant Notice, which costs $39 a year. People in the program receive, by fax or mail, all of the strong specials that we think are worth mentioning.

If we see something that we know is going to be a hot cruise, we notify the customers on our Instant Notice list, who typically receive our mailings in about three or four days. There are rare instances where we will buy something in advance, but that's certainly not the standard way we do business.

Seasons and Expense

Are any particular seasons less expensive for a single? It depends on the destination. If you're talking about the Caribbean, then probably fall would be the softest of seasons. If you're talking about Alaska, of course the solar season would be good, as well as September and October, when it's a little colder still. If you're talking about Europe, it really depends more on the availability of a special offer.

I don't think seasonality is that much of a factor anymore. Vacation periods have spread out. Years ago, the Caribbean season was January, February, and March, and that was it. Now the Caribbean season lasts twelve months a year, and there's as much activity in the Caribbean in June or July as there used to be in February. From that point of view, then, travel has flattened out and therefore it's better, if you're price-conscious, to look for special offers as they come along rather than try to do it season by season. We're all taking more, shorter vacations, and that means that although we may always go away in August every year, we probably go one other week, now, as well.

People are so busy with their schedules and have such intense business lives that it's difficult for people to take two or three weeks in a row. As life gets more intense and pressured, the trend seems to be to break vacations up into shorter periods, such as seven-day cruises instead of fourteen-day cruises or three- or four-day cruises instead of seven-day cruises. This is true not only of cruising, but of vacation travel in general.

Lines, Destinations, and Theme Cruises

What lines are the best for particular destinations? If you asked me four or five years ago to give you a list of the bad lines, it would have been a whole lot easier to do than it is today. What has happened is that there has been a lot of merging of products.

Ships are looking a lot more alike. They're becoming pretty much the same size. They're very similar in design, and the quality has improved dramatically with all the new vessels.

So it's a lot harder today to separate the great ships from the mediocre ships. The truth is, there aren't very many mediocre ships around anymore. It's just gotten too competitive to be that way. There are subtle differences from line to line. Some lines are a little bit more consistent than others, but it's becoming more and more of a parity product.

Just about all of them offer a variety of theme cruises, and they seem to cover everything you could think of: hobbies, celebrity lectures, music, dance, food—you name it, and there's a theme cruise for it. I believe each of the cruise lines have lists of theme cruises in their own brochure, and most of them put out press releases on them. Financial planning, murder mysteries, photography. There's even an O. J. Simpson cruise, since we didn't have enough of it on land. If someone likes country and western dancing or is excited to learn about Normandy from Walter Cronkite, then having that feature enhances the cruise itself.

These features provide just a little extra. Travelers can pick and choose. Such specialty themes are more important in the local cruises than they are for the farther destinations. That is, if you're going to China for the first time, for example, then having a theme cruise will not be that important. On the other hand, if you're going to the Caribbean and you've been to St. Thomas three times, the fact that the cruise is of special interest to you would certainly enhance it.

There are a number of music cruises. Just about all the lines offer chamber music and Cruises of Distinction has put together with Richard Brown of the New York Film Festival a series of film festivals at sea.

Evaluating a Long-Distance Cruise

One subject that is applicable to the single as well as any traveler in general is how to evaluate a long-distance cruise company. There have been some travel scams. If you're dealing with a toll-free number company or a national company of that type, how do you, if you've never dealt with the company before, check it out and make sure that it's legitimate? Here are some things you can do.

The simplest of all is to call the cruise line that you're thinking of booking and say that you're about to purchase a cruise from XYZ company. Can they tell you if the agency you're dealing with is an agency in good standing? Is the company okay to deal with? The cruise line should be able to tell you whether an agency is in good standing. Either they've done business with that company for a long time, or they don't have a record of that agency, or their record indicates that the company is not in good standing.

We offer an executive level of reference with any cruise line that you can think of. For every line, we've got at least one person on the vice presidential level who can vouch for us. This is not an indication of a company's financial status, because any agency, even one in good standing, could go under tomorrow. So it's not 100 percent foolproof, but it's still the simplest thing to do.

You're not dealing with twenty-five cents; you're dealing with twenty-five hundred dollars or twenty-five thousand dollars. With that amount of money at stake, it's worthwhile to deal with a firm that has been around for a while and to make sure that it has a good reputation.

Be sure to get a written invoice *before you pay any money*. The invoice should specify exactly what you were told over the phone. If you are promised a B category single cabin, then that information should appear on the invoice. If the price you were quoted is supposed to include airfare out of Sheboygan, the invoice should reflect that. It should also list anything else you have bought: insurance, shore excursions, and so on.

Check the Better Business Bureau in the city in which the agency is located. The agency ought to be able and willing to give you the number of the local bureau. They funnel all the national complaints from other Better Business Bureaus into the local one. The key question is: Does the agency have outstanding unresolved complaints? Probably any company will have some complaints against it (although I must say during our first eight years in Memphis we didn't have a single one). Once the complaints have been logged in by the Bureau, have they been resolved to the client's satisfaction?

Another means of checking out an agency is getting access to its Dun and Bradstreet (D&B) report. The one thing D&B is useful for is reporting late payments. If the company is behind in any payments, then something is probably wrong.

There are definitely frauds out there. One type advertises and then takes the money and runs. I've run into them, and I have clients who have run into them. Then there are those who are just bad businesspeople, perhaps with good intentions, who take their clients' money and spend it, assuming that more money will be coming in later. They have a slow month, and suddenly they're behind the eight ball and they go out of business—and of course the clients' money goes out of business with them.

Another precaution is to use your credit card in booking. Some people think their credit card automatically means protection, but that's not necessarily so. If you really study it, you'll discover that VISA and MasterCard in particular will squiggle and wiggle out of this so-called protection. When push comes to shove, they will not promise to get your money back.

American Express comes the closest to claiming that it will protect you. Even that company isn't 100 percent, but it's pretty close. At least it provides a third-party advocate if there's a dispute, and a lot of people think that a third party can at least go to bat for you. They do help a little bit, and you have some added weight.

Cruise Insurance

It's not a bad idea to buy cruise insurance, in general. It does cover things like the cruise line or the retailer going belly-up.

It also covers items such as medical and emergency evacuation. Specific terms depend on the type of insurance you buy, and a good retailer can guide you in this matter. Cruises of Distinction promotes Access America, a division of Blue Cross/Blue Shield. You should compare policies. Some cover you only until the day of sailing, for example. Most of them are medically based, which means that the coverage you get from them has to relate to your own medical situation or that of your immediate family.

Overbooking

Overbooking happens. It happens with some frequency. Maybe once a month a line will call us to say that it's overbooked. Usually, the companies handle the situation very well.

They'll tell us to tell clients of a similar sailing on another ship the same week or the following week, and they'll always present an offer. These offers can range from a category upgrade to, in some cases, giving them half the cruise for free. They're usually such generous offers that the whole thing is taken care of very amicably. I can't honestly think of one instance where it hasn't been handled well. In particularly tense situations, the lines will keep upping the offer until everyone is happy. In ten years of business, I've never had a situation in which the cruise line's attitude was "Too bad, you're just out of luck."

People do cancel a lot. We run a cancellation rate of maybe 20 to 25 percent, and the cruise lines may run up to 40 percent.

Category Guarantee

Sometimes, when you call the agency, you may learn that the category you wanted is not available. Perhaps you wanted a category three and there are no more category threes, so the line will give you a guarantee on the category three. The guarantee means that you will get nothing less than the category three, but you have a pretty good chance of getting a higher or better category without any extra charge.

MORE BEST BETS: CRUISE CONSOLIDATORS

The following companies are cruise consolidators. They work the same way that airline consolidators do. Each company tries to sell unsold cabins at deep discounts.

South Florida Cruises
(800) 327-7447

Spur of the Moment Tours & Cruises
(800) 343-1991

OTHER DISCOUNT GROUPS AND CLUBS

The Cruise Line, Inc.
(800) 777-0707

Founded in 1983, this is one of the country's oldest and largest discount cruise and information centers, representing every major cruise line sailing to worldwide destinations. You can save an average of $600 to $2,000 per cabin, even on deluxe, five-star ships. For those who haven't cruised before, call for their *First-Time Cruising Guide*.

Moment's Notice
(212) 980-9550

For a fee of $25 per year, you can get discounts of up to 60 percent. The company acts as a broker between the cruise lines, airlines, and other travel wholesalers.

National Discount Cruise Co.
(800) 788-8108

It discounts all cruise lines and claims to be one of the best cruise discounters in the country. All cruises are sold through its 800 number nationally.

Short Notice Vacations Savings Card
(800) 444-9800

This service is available from Encore for a $36 annual membership fee. You can access the Short Notice Vacation Hotline, which describes last-minute cruises at deeply discounted rates.

Vacations to Go
(800) 338-4962

Find out about discounts on cruise lines via the hotline.

World Wide Cruises
(800) 882-9000

It claims to offer the largest discounts on any ship, anywhere in the world. Discounts available up to 67 percent on selected dates and sailing. Acts as a clearinghouse for all of the major cruise lines. One of the oldest in the nation. You can call to register and receive updates on singles cruises, themes, itineraries, and profiles of ships that best serve singles planning a cruise vacation. It even offers a free cruise-match service for singles who wish to share a cabin for companionship and lower rates.

Worldwide Discount Travel Club
(800) 446-9938

It offers discounts of up to 50 percent on last-minute flights and up to 40 percent off on cruises.

 EVEN MORE BEST BETS

Cruise Only
(800) 209-9871

The Cruise People
(800) 892-7630

Cruise Planners
(800) 385-8233

The Cruise Store
(800) 732-2897; bargain hotline, (413) 525-9004

Discount Cruise Brokers
(800) 682-5122

1-800-TAKE-OFF (yes, that's its name!)
(800) 825-3633

White Travel Service
(800) 547-4790; bargain hotline, (860) 236-6176

World Wide Travel & Cruises
(800) 441-1954

ℬEST BET FALL POSITIONING CRUISES

One of the best-kept secrets in the cruise industry, according to Ann Campbell, Cruise Critic on American Online (AOL), is the great deals available with fall positioning cruises. She says that every fall, ships reposition from Alaska, Europe, New York, and many exotic regions to the winter cruising area. You'll find new and exotic itineraries and some of the best prices of the year on these voyages. Check out Fall Positioning Cruises in the What's New Area on AOL or check with your local travel agent.

ℬEST BET TIPS ABOARD SHIP

- If you want to save money on drinks, stick to ice tea at meals. That's free, along with juices.
- If you want to have your favorite liquor, think about buying a bottle at the next duty-free port and drinking it in your room. Ask if your line allows this.
- The bottled water that is left in your room is not free, so don't open it unless you plan to use it.
- If you want to save money on shore excursions, form your own group and hire a taxi or private car to take you about.

- If you have an on-line service, ask the Cruise Critic on AOL for tips to help you save money while sailing on the high seas.
- Keep a list of your daily charges. You can run up bills very quickly if you don't keep abreast of things.
- Watch for sales on board before buying. Sometimes sales will be towards the end of the cruise or the very last day.
- When on land, carry some of the food from the ship for lunch. Fruits, breads, juices—items that don't need refrigeration. They are especially good for those beach picnics.
- If you do like to have wine at your table, buy an entire bottle. The ship will save what's left and serve it to you each night until it's finished.
- Try buying your own six-packs of soft drinks when you go onshore. Then you can drink them in your room. Every cabin has an ice bucket, which will be refilled daily. You can even take them on shore excursions or to the beach.
- Take your own "portraits" aboard ship. Have a friend or ask someone to take photographs similar to what the ship's photographer is doing. If you must, try to buy them on the very last day, since your choices then would be limited.

APPENDIX

*O*ur Roll Call:
Contact Information

Abercrombie & Kent International
1520 Kensington Road, Suite 212
Oak Brook, IL 60521
(630) 954-2944; outside Illinois (800) 322-7308

If you are interested in Antarctica and prefer a very small ship (53 cabins) with less than 100 passengers, then look into this line. It sails from November through February, with cruises ranging from fourteen to twenty-one days.

Alaska Sightseeing/Cruise West
Fourth and Battery Building, Suite 700
Seattle, WA 98121
(206) 441-8687 or (800) 426-7702

Seven small boats, most of them holding less than 100 passengers, cruise Alaska. This is the largest of the small-ship cruise lines. You will probably find more mature passengers here who love nature, wildlife, and the early sun.

American Canadian Caribbean Line
PO Box 368
Warren, RI 02885
(401) 247-0955 or (800) 556-7450

Small ships with less than 100 passengers each cruise from spring to fall with voyages from six to fifteen days. Cruises the U.S. coastal waterways from Rhode Island and Florida, New England and Canada in the springtime. Various itineraries in the wintertime. Good prices for older, more mature fellow cruisers who favor some adventure. You won't find megaliner glitz here.

American Hawaii Cruises
2 North Riverside Plaza
Chicago, IL 60606
(312) 466-6000 or (800) 765-7000

Carnival Cruise Lines
3655 N.W. 87th Avenue
Miami, FL 33178
(305) 599-2600 or (800) 227-6482

Celebrity Cruises
5201 Blue Lagoon Drive
Miami, FL 33126
(305) 262-8322 or (800) 437-3111

Clipper Cruise Line
7711 Bonhomme Avenue
St. Louis, MO 63105
(314) 727-2929; outside Missouri (800) 325-0010

Club Med Cruises
40 West 57th Street
New York, NY 10019
(800) 258-2633

If you would like a sailing ship combined with diesel power, then you might consider its two ships, *Club Med 1* and *Club Med 2*, each holding upwards of 400 passengers. These deluxe

French ships offer various itineraries, including the Caribbean in the winter.

Commodore Cruise Line
4000 Hollywood Boulevard, Suite 385, South Tower
Hollywood, FL 33021
(954) 967-2100

Two older ships, not megaliners, with good value for first-time cruisers. Both depart from New Orleans, offering seven-day round-trip cruises to the western Caribbean with two alternating itineraries.

Costa Cruises
80 S.W. Eighth Street
Miami, FL 33130
(305) 358-7325 or (800) 462-6782

Crystal Cruises
2121 Avenue of the Stars, Suite 200
Los Angeles, CA 90067
(310) 785-9300

Two luxurious ships, *Crystal Symphony* and *Crystal Harmony*, are highly rated, with the *Harmony* offering cruises from six to twenty-seven days, sailing from Los Angeles and other home ports, depending on the various itineraries. For those who prefer longer cruises, the *Symphony* sails from seven to ninety-six days, including a round-the-world cruise. In the summer, she's in Europe and the Mediterranean; in the winter, the Caribbean.

Cunard
555 Fifth Avenue
New York, NY 10017
(800) 728-6273

Also check out Cunard's Internet address, which is http://
www.cunardline.com.

Delta Queen Steamboat Company
1380 Port of New Orleans Place
New Orleans, LA 70130
(504) 586-0361 or (800) 543-1949

A cruise for those who would like to sail on a classic steamboat
that cruises America's rivers. Cruises year-round on rivers
through Mississippi, Louisiana, Tennessee, Ohio, and Arkansas.

Holland America Line
300 Elliott Avenue West
Seattle, WA 98119
(800) 426-0327

Majesty Cruise Line
PO Box 025420
Miami, FL 33102
(305) 536-0000 or (800) 532-7788

If you are thinking of a shorter cruise, this line has one luxury
ship, the *Royal Majesty,* which leaves from Miami on three- to
four-night cruises to the Bahamas. She sails from October to
May with this itinerary. From May to October, she sails to
Bermuda on six- and seven-night cruises.

Norwegian Cruise Line
7665 Corporate Center Drive
Miami, FL 33136
(305) 436-0866 or (800) 327-7030

Orient Lines
1510 S.E. 17th Street, Suite 400
Fort Lauderdale, FL 33316
(954) 527-6660 or (800) 333-7300

One older luxury ship, recently renovated, holds 800 passengers. Sails to exotic destinations like Antarctica, New Zealand, Australia, the Mediterranean, India, the Indian Ocean, and Southeast Asia/Java Seas.

Premier Cruises
PO Box 025420
Miami, FL 33102
(305) 358-5122 or (800) 222-1003

Three older midsize ships, recently renovated, offer year-round cruises from Miami to the Bahamas, the Caribbean, and the Panama Canal. Low prices, a good value for everyone.

Princess Cruises
10100 Santa Monica Boulevard
Los Angeles, CA 90067
(310) 553-1770 or (800) LOVE-BOAT

Radisson Seven Seas Cruises
600 Corporate Drive, Suite 410
Fort Lauderdale, FL 33334
(305) 776-6123 or (800) 333-3333

For those who want small superdeluxe ships that cruise to different parts of the world. Three ships: *Hanseatic* holds 188 passengers, *Radisson Diamond* holds 354 passengers, and *Song of*

Flower holds 170 passengers. Destinations include the Antarctic, South America, Galapagos, Transcanal, Caribbean, and Asia in the wintertime. In the summer, you will find the ships in the Mediterranean, Europe, Arctic, Iceland, and Greenland.

Royal Caribbean Cruise Lines
1050 Caribbean Way
Miami, FL 33132
(305) 539-6000 or (800) 255-4373

For additional information about Royal Caribbean, visit the line's Internet site of the World Wide Web at www.royalcaribbean.com.

Royal Olympic Cruises (Sun Line Cruises)
1 Rockefeller Plaza
New York, NY 10020
(800) 872-6400

Seabourn Cruise Line
55 Francisco Street, Suite 710
San Francisco, CA 94133
(415) 391-7444 or (800) 929-9595

Three small ships, each carrying around 200 passengers, are the last word in cruising elegance. Very expensive. Varied itineraries include almost three hundred ports in seventy-eight countries. Because of high prices, you will find more of a middle-age or older crowd on board.

Seawind Cruise Line
4770 Biscayne Boulevard, Suite 700
Miami, FL 33137
(305) 573-7447 or (800) 258-8006

Started in 1991. One older ship, recently renovated, sails from Aruba to not-the-usual ports in the southern Caribbean. Sails year-round. Budget prices. Holds a little over 700 passengers.

Silversea Cruises
110 East Broward Boulevard
Fort Lauderdale, FL 33301
(954) 522-4477 or (800) 722-9055

Ultraluxury travel. Two small ships, holding less than 300 passengers. One of the most luxurious lines out there. Started in 1994, its ships carry less than 300 passengers in 148 luxuriously appointed suites. Very expensive, but look for discounts. Because of the high price, you will probably find mostly couples.

Special Expeditions
720 Fifth Avenue, Sixth Floor
New York, NY 10019
(212) 765-7740 or (800) 762-0003

Three older, very small ships holding 37 to 41 passengers. If you like to feel close to nature and very remote ports, look into this line's itineraries, which range from Alaska to South America, the Amazon, and Europe.

Star Clippers
4101 Salzedo Avenue
Coral Gables, FL 33146
(305) 442-0550 or (800) 442-0551

For sailing-ship fans, two four-mast sailing ships hold upwards of 180 passengers each. Sails in the Caribbean and the Mediterranean. Don't worry, though, if there's no wind—each ship has a diesel engine to get through calm days. No casino, no gambling, but lots of fun.

Windjammer Barefoot Cruises
PO Box 190120
Miami, FL 33119
(305) 534-7447 or (800) 327-2601

Windjammer Barefoot Cruises invites you to see your local travel agent for more information.

Windstar Cruises
300 Elliott Avenue West
Seattle, WA 98119
(206) 281-3535 or (800) 258-7245

Windstar Cruises invites you to see your local travel agent for more information. Windstar can be reached on the Internet at www.windstarcruises.com.

World Explorer Cruises
555 Montgomery Street, Suite 1400
San Francisco, CA 94111
(415) 393-1565 or (800) 854-3835

World Explorer Cruises invites you to ask your local travel agent for more information.

OTHER CRUISE LINES

Following are some lesser-known cruise lines and river barges that you may want to look into.

Amazon Tours and Cruises
8700 West Flagler Street
Miami, FL 33174
(305) 227-2266 or (800) 423-2791

Cruise the Amazon from two to six nights.

The Barge Lady
101 West Grand Avenue, Suite 200
Chicago, IL 60610
(312) 245-0900 or (800) 880-0071

For those who would like to cruise on the various canals in
France and England.

Bergen Line
405 Park Avenue
New York, NY 10022
(212) 319-1300 or (800) 666-2374; (800) 323-7436

These cruise ships are European ferries, yet they combine the
size and glamour of oceangoing luxury liners. Sail one day, one
night, or book a tour package through archipelagos and
breathtaking fjords.

Classical Cruises and Tours
132 East 70th Street
New York, NY 10021
(212) 794-3200 or (800) 252-7745

It specializes in various culturally oriented cruises and educational cruises. You will learn, and you won't have to suffer for
lack of creature comforts.

Euro Cruises
303 West 13th Street
New York, NY 10014
(212) 691-2099 or (800) 688-3876; (800) 661-1119

This company line specializes in offbeat European cruises. They
are the American representative for a large number of ships and
riverboats with unusual itineraries.

French Country Waterways
PO Box 2195
Duxbury, MA 02331
(617) 934-2454 or (800) 222-1236

Hilton Red Sea Cruises
c/o Horizon Egypt Company, Hilton Fayrouz,
Naama Bay, Sharm el Sheikh, Egypt

KD River Cruises of Europe
2500 Westchester Avenue
Purchase, NY 10577
(914) 696-3600 or (800) 346-6525 in the east; (800) 858-8587 in the west (includes Hawaii and Alaska)

Cruises the rivers of Europe, also the Volga between St. Petersburg and Moscow.

Mediterranean Shipping Cruises
420 Fifth Avenue
New York, NY 10018
(212) 764-4800 or (800) 666-9333

Nabila Nile Cruises
605 Market Street, Suite 1310
San Francisco, CA 94105
(415) 979-0160 or (800) 443-6453

Cruises the Nile.

Odessa America Cruises
170 Old Country Road, Suite 608
Mineola, NY 11501
(516) 747-8880 or (800) 221-3254

Cruises the rivers, lakes, and canals of Moscow, St. Petersburg.

Regal China Cruises
57 West 38th Street
New York, NY 10018
(212) 768-3388 or (800) 808-3388

St. Lawrence Cruise Lines
253 Ontario Street
Kingston, Ontario, Canada K7L 2Z4
(613) 549-8091 or (800) 267-7868

Spice Island Cruises
c/o Esplanade Tours
581 Boylston Street
Boston, MA 02116
(617) 266-7465 or (800) 426-5492

Swan Hellenic
c/o Classical Cruises
132 East 70th Street
New York, NY 10021
(212) 794-3200 or (800) 220-4789

Cruises of two weeks or longer in Egypt, between Cairo and Aswan. Cruises in the Mediterranean that are culturally oriented.

Viking Star Cruises of Greece
4321 Lakemoor Drive
Wilmington, NC 28405
(910) 350-0100 or (800) 341-3030

TRAVELING THE WORLD ON FREIGHTERS

One day, you might want to fulfill that dream of yours to travel around the world on the high seas. People who travel this way are usually older; many are retired. Many freighters offer amenities and luxuries not found before, and you will meet a hardy breed of cruiser.

The following is a list of some clubs and companies that offer freighter cruises:

Blue Star Pace
c/o TravLtips
PO Box 188
Flushing, NY 11358
(718) 939-2400 or (800) 872-8484

Compagnie Polynesienne de Transport Maritime
2028 El Camino Real South
San Mateo, CA 94403
(415) 574-2575

It offers cruises to Tahiti and surrounding areas.

Freighter Travel Club of America
3524 Harts Lake Road
Roy, WA 98580
(360) 458-4178

Freighter World Cruises
180 South Lake Avenue, Suite 335
Pasadena, CA 91101
(818) 449-3106; fax (818) 449-9573

Call or fax for information about the Freighter Space Advisory. This lists what's available and where. Published every two weeks.

Ivaran Line
111 Pavonia Avenue, Fifth Floor
Jersey City, NJ 07310
(201) 798-5656 or (800) 451-1639

Polish Ocean Lines
c/o Gdynia America Line
1001 Durham Avenue
South Plainfield, NJ 07080
(908) 412-6000, Ext. 107

Freighters leaving from Europe go to the Mediterranean,
Africa, and South America.

TravLtips
PO Box 580188
Flushing, NY 11358
(718) 939-2400 or (800) 872-8584

For a subscription fee of $20, you can get a bimonthly maga-
zine, which reports on the various freighter cruises.

$\mathcal{I}$ndex

Also from Prima

How to Find the Love of Your Life

A Step-by-Step Program That Really Works

Ben Dominitz

U.S. $13.00
Can. $17.95
ISBN: 0-7615-0839-2
paperback / 224 pages

"Whom to call, how to call, what to say, and what to do."
—*Publishers Weekly*

We all know the frustrations and regrets of the dating game: the fear of rejection; the jerks; the awkward, artificial conversations; that sinking, "what-was-I-thinking" feeling. Now there is a better way! Learn how you can:

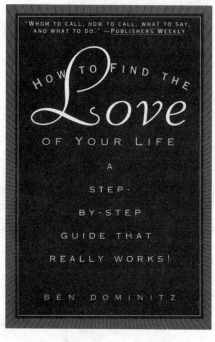

- Master an incredibly effective alternative to the dreaded first date
- Follow the seven-step path to greater intimacy in a new relationship
- And much more!

This groundbreaking book will help you take control of your destiny and find the love of your life!

Visit us online at www.primapublishing.com

Also from Prima

How to Romance the Woman You Love

The Way She Wants You To!

Lucy Sanna
with Kathy Miller

U.S. $12.00
Can. $16.95
ISBN: 1-7615-0870-8
paperback / 224 pages

Find out what women really want in a relationship. The authors share the results of their nationwide survey and reveal women's most intimate desires. This book includes dozens of stimulating strategies and imaginative suggestions to help fulfill the potential of a first date or renew the passion in a lifelong love. Your partner will find you irresistible!

Visit us online at www.primapublishing.com

Also from Prima

How to Romance the Man You Love

The Way He Wants You To!

Lucy Sanna

U.S. $12.00
Can. $16.95
ISBN: 0-7615-0869-4
paperback / 208 pages

Rekindle his passion for romance and learn the truth about what he finds utterly irresistible! Men from all over America reveal their secret soft spots and all the little things that make them go week in the knees.

Visit us online at www.primapublishing.com

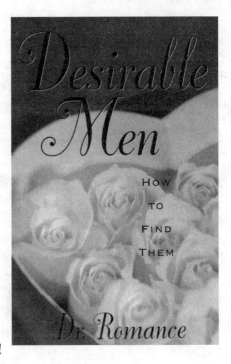

To Order Books

Please send me the following items:

Quantity	Title	Unit Price	Total
_____	How to Find the Love of Your Life	$ _____	$ _____
_____	How to Romance the Woman You Love	$ _____	$ _____
_____	How to Romance the Man You Love	$ _____	$ _____
_____	Desirable Men	$ _____	$ _____
_____	_____	$ _____	$ _____

*Shipping and Handling depend on Subtotal.

Subtotal	Shipping/Handling
$0.00–$14.99	$3.00
$15.00–$29.99	$4.00
$30.00–$49.99	$6.00
$50.00–$99.99	$10.00
$100.00–$199.99	$13.50
$200.00+	Call for Quote

Foreign and all Priority Request orders:
Call Order Entry department
for price quote at 916-632-4400

This chart represents the total retail price of books only (before applicable discounts are taken).

Subtotal $ _____

Deduct 10% when ordering 3-5 books $ _____

7.25% Sales Tax (CA only) $ _____

8.25% Sales Tax (TN only) $ _____

5.0% Sales Tax (MD and IN only) $ _____

7.0% G.S.T. Tax (Canada only) $ _____

Shipping and Handling* $ _____

Total Order $ _____

By Telephone: With MC or Visa, call 800-632-8676 or 916-632-4400.
Mon–Fri, 8:30-4:30.
WWW: http://www.primapublishing.com

By Internet E-mail: sales@primapub.com
By Mail: Just fill out the information below and send with your remittance to:

**Prima Publishing
P.O. Box 1260BK
Rocklin, CA 95677**

My name is _____

I live at _____

City _____ State _____ ZIP _____

MC/Visa# _____ Exp. _____

Check/money order enclosed for $ _____ Payable to Prima Publishing

Daytime telephone _____

Signature _____